Ecstatic Playground

Ecstatic Playground

Creating as Gods and Masters on the Playground of Life

Allison Holley

Author photo by Kim Awa
www.kimniawa.com

ISBN-13: 979-8-9888792-2-0
ISBN-13: 979-8-9888792-1-3
ISBN-13: 979-8-9888792-0-6

Dedication

I dedicate this book to each of you: playful beings and pioneers
of the New Frequencies.

Thank you for playing this divine game with me.

Table of Contents

Foreword

In 2018, just a few days after I published my first book, The Era of the True Creator, I received a download for an "assignment" to begin writing this book.

I wrote down on a sticky note:
How can I play more with this? Study play. This is what your next book is about.

I of course thought I had absolutely won the life lottery. My assignment was to study play? Sign me up! I was anticipating the joy, ease, and flow of fun times ahead.

I have to laugh about it now (the playful laugh of a madwoman!), because what followed for the next several years was a study into why so many of us often don't play, and what makes it so hard for us all to be playful with life.

Unwittingly, I fell into the illusions of being oh so human. Immersed in these human realms, I studied control, limitation, and fear. I studied people-pleasing and giving my power away. I studied confusion and helplessness. And about six months before I finished writing this book, I reached one particularly low point where I was so lost in misery and disconnected from my god-self that I wanted to die.

But in these years, I also experienced the richness of being human. I studied the human dramas of love and connection with "others." I learned more and more to be in my body and to ground and connect with the earth. I learned to channel joyful energy through my physical body for the various types of play that only a human can experience: laughter, sex, ecstasy, connection with nature, playful movement and dancing…

And my abilities to be multidimensional, to consciously move among the realms and dimensional spaces we occupy in this human experience, and to channel insights and teachings from higher frequencies massively grew. It was as if, in the exploration of the depths of the human realms, I had created a slingshot into the truth of who I am. I am both human and cosmic, and I am able to play within many dimensions and realms—though now with greater consciousness than before.

I would not have been able to write this book without a full descent into unconscious play. For all of this exploration, and for all those who were with me on the journey, I am overwhelmingly grateful.

Introduction: The Void

The following comes from a channeling session I was offering a client and friend, wherein a vision of the deeper truth of creation was shown to me. I entered the origin of creation and was shown that we are each prisms, and as conduits of creation, we draw light from the Void and fractalize it through ourselves. This vision was pure poetry, and it made sense to me on a level that is beyond human—and even beyond our understanding of ourselves as beings. Our true essence is closer to conscious sacred geometry. I have included this explanation here, to open us to awaken to these higher truths.

All creation emerges from the Void.

All That Is, exists in the Void. It is the Void.

The Void IS, and infinite potential is derived from it.

The light is simply what we see.

Within quantum perception, we begin to understand that something exists when we look at it. This is how we are creators: as humans we are able to perceive the light that emanates from the Void. We are both the projectors of the light, and the ones that perceive it.

Perceiving the light is our ability to see this physical reality and to play within it.

Becoming more light means that we are drawing more of the fullness of this projected energy into our physical reality.

Enlightenment means to channel the fullest capacity of light that is available to us. We are the light bearers. Our work as creators is to allow this light to come through us, and also to perceive it.

The light is the manifestation into the physical. To create means to bring forth our chosen light from the Void. The light is how we see, within our physical world, what we have chosen. But the light is only a fractal, a partial projection from the Void.

As we draw from the infinite possibility of the Void, we act as a prism for the light that comes through our being. In the prismatic fractaling that occurs through ourselves, we have a spectrum of colors available to us, which we can use to paint our new creations. We are artists of life, painting the picture as we step into it, choosing the colors and even the palette with which we paint. And our painting will never be fully finished, for as we create, we are moving and shifting the colors continuously to create the next layer of our painting.

To be masterful creators, we need to honor the Void from which everything comes. To honor the Void means to become conscious of our infinite nature and our infinite level of choice. It means to make a conscious choice about what we bring to light, about what we create. When we honor the Void, we tap into our ability to make anything become light, which means to make anything manifest.

Many of us choose unconsciously because we don't recognize that we are the creators, we are the projectors of what we choose from within the Void. But it is the choosing, the focusing, that is the fun in the human experience. In this choosing, and in our mastery over this choosing, we find so much joy. We can play—being within the All That Is—while still projecting our chosen reality within this human landscape. In this play, we become consciously multidimensional and exist in multiple landscapes simultaneously. We are being the All That Is, as a focused moment in time.

We are a creation of the All, and so also, we are the Void: the Everything and the Nothing.

In this game of being human, we fall under illusions because of our limited ability to perceive All That Is. One of the main illusions we experience comes from our focus on the light. Our human experience has trained us to believe that Light is all there is, that only manifest form is real, and that only the known spectrum of colors is "good." In our human experience, we tend to only see what comes from the Void; we see the externalization of the Void. But the Void is All That Is; it is perfect creation. This includes the All and the Nothing, the Void and the Light.

Through ascension, we consciously expand beyond this duality. There is no imbalance when we allow All That Is. We become the All That Is, merging with it once again. Our acceptance of everything will not only allow in what we may have been pushing away or what we perceive to be undesirable;

it will bring everything into balance. We become one with the fabric of the All That Is, which pulls nothing in and pushes nothing away.

When we agree to allow in the All That Is, we bring balance to the light and darkness within our own being and our perception of reality. Duality is transmuted into a balance of polarities. This is why black is a color of mastery, a sacred color. Ancient cultures venerated the dark but also feared it, because in those times we weren't capable of recognizing our full potential beyond duality. When we can cease to be afraid of the dark, we recognize our limitless potential as creator gods.

And yet we are still in the mode of creation as humans, playing within duality and a time-based reality. We perceive ourselves to be in one moment in time, instead of experiencing everything as now. We vacillate between polarities in order to experience one polarity and then manifest from it. The process becomes a cycle: we experience, then manifest; experience, then manifest. We are essentially drawing from the Void to project light; or more accurately, we are in the Void and choosing, and then projecting light. We do this unconsciously, which keeps us bound to a dualistic process of creation that seems to be beyond our control.

To become masters in these realms, then, we must learn to consciously exist in, and draw from, the Void. Through this practice, we see that presence moves us beyond duality. Presence is our access to the Void, and thus to creation itself. In true creation, we experience a quantum level of presence. We have a balanced perception of polarities and are able to simultaneously exist in the Void and project the light that we choose.

This is why so many who have reached this level of wisdom are quiet. They allow themselves to be highly present and exist in the Void, understanding that there is a tremendous amount of power and oneness in this place. They allow themselves to be the prismatic creators who bring forth all creation from the Void—and they do so with a deep sense of peace, free of the attachments created by the illusion of duality or separation.

When we step beyond duality and the illusion that the Light is all there is, we understand that the fullness of this life experience is fun for us—even the confusion, even the unconscious choices and the experiences that we perceive to be painful. And to consciously choose what we desire is incredible ecstasy. As prisms of light bringing creations forth from the Void, this is our play.

Play

From a cosmic perspective, nothing is ever necessary. It is all only ever play.

As incarnated beings in our current world, we tend to think of play as something "extra." We think of play as recreation, something we engage in when our work is done; or we disregard it altogether as silly or immature, as something that only children do.

But this is all a limited conception of the truth of play. Play is our very existence. It is actually what we're doing here on Earth all the time.

In this human experience, we are constantly playing in infinite ways. We are playing with our energetic creation and with our ability to channel these energies into physicality. We are playing with the creation of ourselves and our personality, and with how these interface with our projected world. We are playing with perception, our ideas of reality, and our mastery in these realms. Everything we do is play—a play of creation and light as it dances through dimensions.

But just because we're playing doesn't necessarily mean we're having fun. Our level of consciousness is what determines how much we enjoy this play.

When we are unconscious, play feels like work; it feels like pain and suffering, like drama. Life lived unconsciously feels like a "test." But life is never a test. It is a game, a theatrical play in which we are the directors. When our energy and actions come from the consciousness of our highest selves, play is an experience that is joyful, creative, and endlessly entertaining and fun.

By expanding our perception of play, we gain a new understanding of what it means to have fun from a higher-self perspective. "Fun" does not necessarily mean satisfying the ego through known activities or experiences; it means seeking new experiences and having new challenges present themselves. From a cosmic perspective, we like challenges in our play. What is fun from a cosmic perspective is to explore outside the bounds of the human mind; things that are fun on this level may therefore seem confusing to us on a human level.

Even when examined from a purely human perspective, we can recognize that play is a fundamental human need. It is what we live for, once our basic physical survival needs are met. And this continues through our awakening: when we are conscious beyond the world of polarities and have realized our eternal nature, playful creation and mastery within these realms are the next steps. We play outside of the game of right and wrong, and our choices are motivated by the desire to learn, experience and consciously create what we want to play with. Play is what we exist to do when we know we are eternal beings.

Play in all forms is natural and fundamental, one of the basic elements of our being. So why don't we know how to do it? Why don't we effortlessly play in life?

The answer is that we have all created many boundaries around acceptable ways to play and limitations around what play can be. We often take things so seriously and make life so complicated, that it's hard to know where to begin.

Sometimes we don't play because we don't feel we deserve to—as if we need to earn our right to play. We feel the need to apologize for the joy that we have.

And sometimes we are threatened by play. Play may feel chaotic to those whose worlds are built so strictly from the mind, because mental constructs fall apart when things seem to be out of order or control. Or play may feel uncomfortable, because it involves unlearning so many self-imposed limitations—such as our ideas of perfection and our dualistic beliefs of right and wrong. To those who are still enmeshed in the dualistic realms, play could seem unnecessary at best, and selfish at worst. But these perceptions come from our ego and not from our higher self.

Most people in the world now are feeling a certain level of discomfort with the massive changes that are rapidly occurring, as old structures break down and a new multidimensional landscape is created. With all the shifts and chaos right now, Many will think, "How do we justify playing in a time like this? How do we allow ourselves to feel comfortable playing, when play seems to be some sort of a privilege in the midst of so much suffering?"

The cosmic truth is that now is the perfect time for play. In fact, play is especially important in times when the world may feel chaotic and heavy. And though the world may seem chaotic right now, what we perceive as chaos is misunderstood. Chaos is not the opposite of peace, but it is an amplified extreme. Much like the friction within an explosive, the energy of so much chaos is the birthplace that creates an explosion of consciousness, or what we know of as awakening. This may seem very uncomfortable, but it is for a beautiful purpose: to inspire us all to create from a new level. At this new level, we exist in love and learn to play in physical reality with freedom and self-mastery. And as a collective, we have never been more ready than we are now for this exact level of creation.

It takes a brave person to allow themselves to play in a world where so many people see suffering as noble. And for those who are ready to move into that landscape of play, learning not to care how other people view us is actually part of our journey toward play. We must recognize that if people can't or choose not to see from this higher perspective, that is their choice, and there's nothing we need to do about it. This act of letting go of what others may think or feel about us may be uncomfortable, but this discomfort is the fertile friction that helps us move to the next level of consciousness; this is our awakening. And when we no longer live in chaos or fear, allowing ourselves to play is the next step.

Through all this transition, we can be gentle with ourselves. We are learning a completely new way of being, and so we can be curious and open as we discover new realms of possibility and begin to create in a new way. When feelings of struggle arise, we can ask, "How can I play more with this?" We don't have to follow the old paradigm, and we don't have to believe anyone who tells us not to play, not to be joyful, or not to trust ourselves as we step into self-mastery.

We are here on the planet at this time to explore boundaries and open them up, and to create in greater magnitude. We are here to love on an expanded level, for love is the pinnacle within this human experience; in truth, love is all that is. It is the All That Is.

Play is letting go of the mental struggle, or the illusion of struggle. Play is standing still and commanding the energies around us. Play is consciously choosing our reality. Play is consciously engaging with different realms of reality. Play, simply put, Is. Just as We Are. Just as I Am.

How absolutely in love can we be with being? How fun can we make this life, this moment in time, this human body, this density realm, this physical experience? How much can we enjoy the illusions we are playing within? How much can we love and appreciate the full breadth and depth of this moment, and then consciously choose what we'd like to create next? Can we dive into this moment and make it even bigger? Can we experience ecstasy by going deeper in this moment—not by leaving it or being above it, but by being fully embodied in it, right here and now?

Our work is to play. We have to play. It is the inevitable next frontier.

This is our sacred mission. Not just to have knowledge, but to have joy, too. Not just to awaken, but to play.

Multidimensional Awareness

Consciousness is rapidly shifting in our current times, and we are collectively expanding. At this time, many beings on the planet wish to further their knowledge of what it means to be within this human existence, and also conscious within the higher-frequency realms.

There is much talk of entering the fifth dimensional consciousness; however, describing ourselves or these realms in such an overly simplistic way does not work. In creating terminology, the human mind inevitably encapsulates ideas and holds them in stasis. But nothing is truly static.

We are all multidimensional and always shifting and playing with the world at different levels of consciousness, along a spectrum from unconscious to hyper-conscious. There are many aspects of ourselves that are operating from a fifth dimensional perspective, and beyond. We also have parts of ourselves that are operating in lower realms. So rather than defining the fifth dimension, it is clearer to say that we are learning to consciously enter the quantum realms and even play beyond them.

In our ascension, we begin to see that we exist within all realms at once—the human realms, the star realms, and the many realms in between. This is the case even if we have not been actively playing within them because of our limited awareness. In truth, we have been playing human all our lives, and thus playing small by default. Through awakening, we are simply releasing those confines. We are now playing with a more expanded consciousness while existing in human form. This recognition is our progression toward multidimensional awareness.

This is a higher level of play than what we've experienced before. It is wizardry and mastery; we are playing with our mastery over the lower realms because our conscious perception is within the higher realms. This is the play of True Creation.

Living multidimensionally is like playing on a giant checkerboard with multiple frequency tiers. On one tier of this checkerboard is the human perspective. If we move up a tier, we enter the game of our psychic energy, where our thoughts, emotions, dreams, and our perception of time as we know it are created. Beyond that is the quantum tier, and beyond that, we exist in the prismatic rainbow frequencies of the sixth dimension. We are learning to play the games of each of these dimensions, and to gain more consciousness in all of them so that we can play more adeptly. In conscious play, we activate our mastery.

More consciousness means more play: the more consciousness we have in different realms, the more we can play in them. And with more consciousness, apparent limitations become the parameters for a game. When we know the rules of any given realm, we can then consciously play with them. This play can include bending time, manifesting more clearly, or even manipulating physicality and the material world to match our desires. On the other hand, when we are less conscious, we are unaware of other levels of reality beyond the physical. And if we aren't aware that something exists, how can we play with it?

When we consciously engage with life from higher-frequency realms, the game becomes more playful and fun. This is because it is much easier to make big shifts and movements from the realms where matter doesn't matter. Consciously creating from the sixth dimension is pure play.

This is not to say that life ceases to give us areas of friction as we gain consciousness—and it doesn't mean that people within a certain realm of reality don't experience pain. What this really means is that there are different choices available based on the level of game that we're playing. And based on the level we are playing on and consciously operating from, the friction we may experience changes and the quality of the lessons we learn varies.

The ease of existence within higher-frequency states may lead us to think that they are better. We may even wish that we could avoid engaging in the human or astral realms, as the lack of clarity in these realms can cause us to feel stuck or unable to make a conscious choice. But we are never stuck. And there is nothing wrong with any of these realms. We are playing, and learning to master our ability to choose the realm that we want to play in and operate from.

We are often confused as to what it means to move into higher-frequency states. We may think that developing in our spiritual consciousness means that we are "better" or somehow more "perfect," or that we are "saving the world." But actually, all of those measurements fall away as we continue to awaken to higher-frequency truths. In becoming conscious as humans within higher-frequency realms, we see that this is all a game that no one can lose.

Also, we often fail to recognize the absolute perfection and beauty of the human perspective. Becoming consciously multidimensional shows us that our spiritual selves and our human selves are not separate, and that one is not better than the other. Even when we have impulses that come from the human perspective, they are perfect and perfectly fine to act upon. Our spirituality includes everything that we are—even our basest desires—because it is our spirit manifesting in all its various fractal forms.

There is no hierarchy. All is in perfect order, beyond the confines of the mind's perception. No one really needs to be anywhere, and nothing needs to exist in any particular form or function. It is all a matter of choice. As eternal creators, we get to choose what's going to entertain us the most. No matter which realm we're playing in, the joy is in our conscious choosing of it.

Sometimes we even choose to be unconscious in order to walk the path our soul has set out for us, because if we were more conscious, we would choose a different path and not learn the specific lesson that our soul is calling in. In fact, if we were more conscious, the choice of chaos or pain wouldn't even exist in our world, because these experiences are perceptions only held within lower frequencies. Different layers of reality offer different experiences, and we can't see these experiences—they don't even exist for us to choose them—until we perceive those realms of reality.

In denser realities—such as the human experience—our perception and awareness slow down, making it easier for us to forget who we are and to become myopic and sluggish in our learning. This is much like the pressure and slow movement of being deep underwater, versus the ease of movement closer to the water's surface. For some, the density and heaviness feels uncomfortable or unfamiliar. This is especially true if we are used to lighter frequencies and haven't played within the Earth realm many times before. But even though it may be different or uncomfortable, there is nothing wrong with this density. It is simply a part of the experience that we're going through as incarnated humans playing within the parameters of this frequency realm. With expanded consciousness, we learn how to celebrate all experiences.

But in this awakening age, the whole planet is changing and going through a massive expansion, and higher frequencies are constantly streaming in. It is becoming uncomfortable to be as dense as we have been in the past. This frequency shift is happening rapidly, and we feel it palpably. In fact, if we were to travel back in time 100 years, we'd feel miserably dense! Even just a century ago, human consciousness was vibrating noticeably slower. As the planet ascends, we are experiencing condensed learning and condensed time, and we are each vibrating at higher and higher frequencies.

As we increasingly know ourselves as energetic beings, we no longer feel bound by the laws of matter. We learn to guide and direct physicality, because we know that the energetic laws are what command the physical laws, and not the other way around. By trusting our own infinite nature, we more fully trust the infinite nature of the Universe, and that anything we ask for will come to us. Our play is now to point and command things into existence, to use the tools of energy to adjust the illusion of physicality and to joyfully create.

In quantum reality, the space between our human self and our higher self closes, and we begin to navigate our lives from our higher-self consciousness. Quantum consciousness is the I AM consciousness: I AM what I desire; I AM the All That Is. With this awareness, we want for nothing; everything is accessible to us when we simply bring our conscious awareness to it. Our intentions can manifest as quickly as we allow them to—even instantly, if we are highly present.

It is fun to learn this new playing field—to learn how to barely move and let the world move for us. But it is still unknown territory for us, and so it takes practice. We are used to the old way of trying, pushing, and moving the gears in a system; we are used to the machine stopping when we stop trying to move those gears. We are used to flexing our muscles and doing things with all of our might, and using the energy of physicality to move things. And now we're learning to play with quantum energy, which creates massive change simply through consciousness and intention.

Playing in these higher realms is supposed to be easy for us. And it's going to be easy for us. That being said, we will likely still encounter moments in which things don't seem to be working. But even in these moments, we can be easy about it. We can be in our heart and trust that we are guided and given everything that we need. We can trust that in our growing awareness and our more multidimensional perspective, we will see opportunities that we couldn't previously see.

Gods On Earth

As we collectively elevate beyond our old paradigms, we are each beginning to see and understand the extent of our abilities to create. We are each awakening to our next level of consciousness, and for those who are ready, this means recognizing ourselves as gods.

The word or notion of "god" has many possible meanings. Here we use this word in two ways: the first is in reference to ourselves as the creator of our reality. The second is the aspect of god as an omniscient parental figure who holds an understanding of how all things work. To know ourselves as gods means that we begin to play with expanded creator abilities and with the sovereignty of self-governance. As gods, we are consciously creating our individual reality—and thus the collective reality—through our multidimensional play.

Everyone is playing a game. And yet, there are many who are still not awakened to this awareness. Many people are still unconscious in their creations, and are therefore looking for a god external to themselves—an all-knowing being—to both create the collective reality and show how to navigate it. Those of us who are masters of our own reality are creating games that others can play in, until they too learn how to consciously create.

The idea of knowing ourselves as gods may be uncomfortable for many people. There is a belief that if we know ourselves as gods, we take on a power that is beyond human capacity. We may believe that being in the fullness of our power will make us domineering, or that we will use that power to hurt other people. Many may even feel that it is dishonest to create a reality that others experience, or that in doing so, we are taking away another person's free agency or being manipulative.

But creating a reality for others to look toward is not manipulative. Instead, it is based on a level of presence and expanded consciousness. It is based on a core of deep love, which comes from knowing the truth of the new light vibration that we are holding. This is not "truth" as in objective reality, nor is it "truth" as opposed to any falsehood. From a higher vibrational perspective, Truth means frequency alignment. As gods, we understand that to be in our truth means to hold the vision of our own reality and to create from this state. Even though we know that no objective reality ever exists, we recognize that we are creating the truth all the time, and that there is also a core Truth of harmonic alignment.

Recognizing that we are the gods and creators of our own reality is not egotistical, either; it actually right-sizes our responsibility in life. Seeing that we are gods means that we know we are responsible for ourselves, and that everyone else is also responsible for themselves.

Yet so many of us, on a subconscious level, are afraid of moving into the higher-frequency realms of play and knowing ourselves as gods. Memories from our collective human history are blocking us.

Before the vibrations of the Earth and people shifted into our current age of awakening, there were two distinct paths one could take upon becoming enlightened and awakening to god consciousness. The first path was to live as a detached observer, shutting oneself off from the world. This was non-confrontational and even pleasant, as there is a level of entertainment in observation, in perceiving the chaos that other people are experiencing. This is why so many masters before us remained in this perfect observer role—in long meditation, witnessing everything, and feeling the bliss of observation from a place of non-attachment.

The second possible path after enlightenment, the alternative to shutting oneself away and observing the dramatic creations of others, was martyrdom. This was because those who reached enlightenment would try to go back into the world and teach what they had come to understand. But the state of the world and the consciousness of the collective was too dense. These enlightened beings would try to teach what they had come to know, and even though it would help many people, the collective at the time were not ready to know themselves in this way; they still saw their power as being external to themselves. Those who understood themselves to be creators were a threat to the foundations of the collective reality, and were often killed or cast out of society for their knowledge.

Martyrdom is very strong in our past; it is embedded in us that people could be so uncomfortable with us for having a higher-frequency awareness that they would want to kill us. But that is a paradigm of the past. We are now collectively reaching consciousness within higher-dimensional realms. Now, we have the ability to take these truths, this understanding of ourselves as gods and creators, and also play. We no longer need to be martyrs. Instead, we will find that others are grateful that we hold this truth, because they themselves are also coming to know it and are looking for guidance.

Knowing ourselves as gods is like being a loving parent; in the same way that children struggle to do something that adults can easily do, others are naturally going to look to us as if we have more power, because we operate at a frequency in which life moves more easily. This is where we understand god consciousness to be the same as universal love. We come to see that opening to more of the truth of who we are inherently means that we are connecting to the divine source of love, and that we are agreeing to more and more of ourselves as that love. God is love. As gods, we are divine love, embodied.

As the illusions of our world begin to fall apart, many people who do not feel comfortable holding their own power will look for another god or parental figure in whom to place their trust. Some people have looked to the government or to their community to be in this parental role. For many of those people, that security is falling apart intensely right now. For others, their "god" or sense of reliability and stability is in finances; they rely on the known structures within the financial world for a sense of control. For those who are very worried about healthcare and place this care solely in the hands of others, their "god" is science and doctors. And for still others, their "god" is in their partnerships and relationships, as they depend on their perception of someone loving them in order to feel safe and secure.

But we're at a point where we're no longer able to look to other people, the government, science, or anything external for validation. Anything that is outside the truth of our infinite nature is being stripped away from each of us. This serves to help us find our own inner freedom, and recognize ourselves as creators within this existence. In order to fully claim our own sovereignty and step into our god-selves, all of these externalizations of power need to fall away.

What will emerge from the changes, if we allow it to, is something even more true: our own inner strength. This is not human inner strength or psychological inner strength, but the infinite within each of us—which is the real higher power. Through these shifts, we become aware that our own inner journey has nothing to do with anyone else's. We do not worry about other people's views or about what they're doing or perceiving. We are all simply playing our own games.

As gods, our work is to get very clear with our personal truth, finding the core of light within ourselves and operating from it. Knowing our own truth through the prism of play will allow each of us to be clear in what we wish to create.

Many people's fears are being activated at this time, because as the higher-frequency energy of change filters into lower consciousness, it changes our foundational structures. This is like a seismic shift, wherein the movement that occurs under the surface causes huge movements on the earth above it. We're experiencing a shift that is felt throughout many dimensions. In the higher frequencies, these changes feel adventurous, interesting, and exhilarating. But from the perspective of our ego and lower frequencies, the changes feel threatening, and they engender defensive attitudes as many people fight to maintain what they know and understand.

As the world shifts, many people will completely wear themselves out from the fear, anger, sadness, and frustration of trying to fix the old structures that are burning down—instead of allowing them to fall apart as they are meant to.

Powerful shifting is occurring in the fourth dimension, or the astral realms, as well. Some people, as they awaken, witness the fight between good and evil that is occurring on the astral realms. This can often be seen as angels and demons fighting, or the "good" spiritual beings fighting against the "bad"— which people often interpret to be a "war in Heaven."

But this concept of a "war in Heaven" is a flawed understanding. War is indeed a part of physical reality; it is what happens when we create from effort and come up against something and need to push or use force. In the higher realms, which operate under the quantum laws of oneness, there is nothing to fight against, and so how can there be a war? If we never need to push, if reality literally responds to our joyful creative impulse, there is no war. There is dancing, movement, and ease. And so we can see that our perception of a war in Heaven is actually a war within the astral realms, created by our own mental projections that have taken form.

The attachment to fighting a war or being a warrior exists for people who appreciate being able to use resistance to feel themselves—because it feels more real to push against something. It can be helpful to know that within this physical reality there is always some amount of resistance. As energy transfers from the quantum reality into the physical reality, it is met with the resistance of denser energy. This resistance doesn't have to be like slogging through mud, though, and it doesn't have to bring out our warrior. It can be lighter—more like swimming and less like moving through brick walls, more

22

like flying through water particles and less like hacking through a glacier.

We can choose to maintain our consciousness in the astral realm and feel the war, tension, inner chaos and fear—and there is nothing wrong with that choice. But it will become harder to hold those vibrations as the planet ascends. And when we choose to operate from a quantum perspective, we will discover an ease of movement, even within the denser realms we are playing within.

Operating as gods means that we are highly conscious within the higher- or expanded-frequency realms, and therefore are not wrapped up in dualistic drama. When we know we are gods, we no longer externalize our power or fight against something outside of ourselves that we perceive to be "bad." Instead, we accept everything.

As gods, we know that we are free, and we are playing in this freedom of creation. When others see this freedom within us, a common perspective we might hear is: "Why don't you care? Why aren't you fighting the 'good' fight? Why aren't you worried about the world, like I am?" We might feel misunderstood for not diving into the fear, chaos, and drama when we are around people who are still only conscious within dualistic realms.

But soon, people will be desperate for anyone who can hold a perspective outside of the drama. People will be seeking out individuals who are not enmeshed in it. Practicing being outside of that space now is going to be of huge service to others, as we all continue to awaken.

We are each being upgraded within our DNA spiral, and as this upgrade occurs, shifts within the human sphere are inevitable. Many civilizations fall when genetic upgrades occur, because the systems that were built no longer serve this newly evolved human. It is helpful to know this, so we can see that no one is causing this chaos to occur. And yet since it is occurring, there is a desire to find fault amidst all of the destruction.

We can cease to find fault in the destruction, and even in the people who are holding onto the old patterns, or who are purposefully trying to stall human development. By turning our awareness within and knowing our true power, we also place our focus on the creation of the New.

What a powerful ability we have, what powerful gifts each of us has: to be stable in the vibrational frequencies of the New in the midst of all that is happening in the world. While so many people in the world are paying attention to or are distracted by the old structures that are falling, we are actively seeking and creating the new world we inhabit. We will see bright, new, beautiful creations that we ourselves mold. And we see the path that we choose with increasing clarity, cultivating our understanding of how to be conscious creators, gods, and masters.

We are meant to be leaders and guides here, each in our own way. This does not necessarily mean that each individual will be public about it; but through our gentle example, others will surely see us. As we shine more brightly, it is important to be aware that others will see us and wish to be like us, and they may also feel conflicted about how this looks in their own lives. This will make some people angry. It will make others jealous. Many people will feel confused by the "new" reality that we are creating—which has always been reality within a certain frequency. These are signs that we have ignited something that is actually positive, that is meant for everyone's benefit.

While many people feel stuck in difficult, heavier emotions, these are really catalysts for their growth and awakening. In moments in which we recognize these emotions in others and even in ourselves, it is important to have the compassion of a true Ascended Master, the compassion of seeing and knowing that we all simply wish to understand our own mastery and channel it through our being. It is hard for many people to move past their own perceived limitations and step into their personal mastery. But it is possible for us all. Everyone is receiving help from their guides and their own internal divinity. Our job as incarnated beings is to hold this light frequency within ourselves as much as we can—not to attenuate our own energy to make others feel more comfortable.

In this new era, anything is possible. We are creators, playing consciously with our creations; and as highly conscious creators, we know ourselves better than anyone else can know us. We know our capacity for creation and magic, and we know the perfect design for each of our individual lives. We trust ourselves to know, feel, and sense the direction in which we are each guided. As creators, gods and masters, things begin to look and feel very different. Within the vestiges of the old world, we are creating the New.

Time

In higher realms, everything is here and now, and all possibilities exist. But as part of the game of physicality, we get to play within a time-based reality.

As humans, we perceive time as a linear model. We move through the fabric of time and experience events as they unfold, from the past into the future. The unfolding of time is largely what the human experience is about: feeling and experiencing moments. And this is fun, because within this perception we make so many new discoveries. In the unfolding of time we get to make choices—one decision, one moment, one probable causality to be walked at a time—and then be within the experience that these choices bring. When we know from our higher perspective that everything is occurring at once, the human perception of time is so delicious, and we see it as an incredible gift.

As we continue to ascend, life lived solely from the human perspective starts to feel heavy. On the physical plane we are at the mercy of time, and from this perspective there is so much to manage. We push and pull, using physicality to move physicality. But in our awakening, we discover a lighter way of operating.

From a higher frequency, we understand that time is relative, and that we can manipulate it. Time is an illusion, a continuum of a moment that can be as long or as short as we want it to be. It is like a slinky that we can compress or elongate according to our own desires. This example illustrates that time is a toy, rather than something serious that controls our existence. With this new understanding, timelines become more open, and there is ample opportunity in this expansion to explore and play. The future and the past are seen to be ideas and constructs. We begin to understand that not only can we create the future, we can also change the past—because what we call a "memory" is only an idea, and ideas can be changed at any moment.

From the awareness that all moments are now, we can see that everything in existence has already played out in its fullness in all directions of time. When all moments are now, the soul has already reached its perfectly exalted state, yet still desires to perpetuate its discovery as a game. Presence is our gateway to this truth. It is our access to the realms of the eternal Now. Being in a state of presence becomes a quantum, psyche-shifting experience that reverberates throughout our whole being and fills us with ecstasy. From a deep level of presence, we can know eternity.

In the perception that all is now, everything that we wish for has already occurred. The process of conscious manifestation is merely aligning with this knowledge. Quantum time is literally instantaneous, because everything exists now. With this understanding, we see that all physical reality instantly aligns with our internal perception, and the timing of the unfolding of events is only based on the time it takes for us to align internally. But our work to more fully align does not involve grasping to attain a certain vibration, but rather letting go to

allow our natural vibration to exist. We live fully in our purpose and in our joy now, because now is all that is.
In physical reality, where we are influenced by the structure and rules of the external world, we see time as being based on actions that create results. We believe: "If I do x, then y happens." From this perspective, we feel like we have to follow a schedule. We believe that unless we follow the structure that the outside world is showing us, what we need and desire won't come to us.

For many of us, our mind still believes in "right timing"—the idea that there is a perfect time for something to happen that is beyond our control and external to our consciousness. The truth that we discover from a quantum perception is that the timing of events is based on how quickly we allow something to occur without a mental struggle to block it. It is more helpful to think of "vibrational timing" rather than "divine timing," as this connects us to the truth that our vibrational alignment determines the flow of our experiences.

The belief that the Universe operates with a cosmic timing that acts upon us is one way we justify holding something away from ourselves, which reinforces the illusion that our power is external to us of the externalization of our power. We can see this most clearly when we can command one thing into our life instantly, with no struggle; and yet in other areas of our life, our ability to intentionally create seems to lag behind. This dissonance happens because of our dissonant beliefs, not because of a universal structure of time.

In quantum reality, the inner structure is all that matters. Our desired creations can manifest immediately; or if our inner structure is calibrating to our desires, this process can take a little bit longer. Likewise, when we are in alignment with our truth, we compress timelines, and when we are living in drama, we re-loop and elongate timelines. We know we are re-looping when, instead of letting things flow, we hold on to an idea or past moment and try to recreate it.

When all things exist in one moment and we can access anything from the All, the timing in which something occurs is always based on our allowance of it to come to us. Thus, our ability to play in quantum consciousness is really about learning to receive. And in learning to receive, it is our self-worth that determines how quickly we are able to manifest our desires. Building self-love and thereby self-trust will bring us into the frequency of receiving, as we will know we are worthy of all that we desire.

We are commanding all of our reality, whether we are fully conscious of it or not. Sometimes we unconsciously don't allow instant manifestations to occur within this physical reality because of the game that we're playing with ourselves. We like to watch things unfold over time, and we enjoy the mystery of the movement of it—even if we don't consciously know it. Even the spaces between the manifestation of our desires are moments that we want to experience. We enjoy the play of denying ourselves everything we desire at once, and witnessing the unfolding.

Many of us also block the perception that "all is now" due to a fear of boredom. We unconsciously fear that we'll be bored if we aren't waiting or yearning for things to occur. Boredom is a terrifying concept for the mind, and when we begin to step into these higher-frequency realms, it often looms as a possible experience in our expansion. We often unconsciously create drama to stall the process of everything occurring at once, and to re-loop what we already perceive and understand. This reveals our conflicting desires: on the one hand, to play within the human sphere of drama and re-looping in order to experience time, and on the other hand, to play within the infinite, as it silently calls us into our expansion.

But there is a huge gap between our mental conception of infinity, and the actual, profoundly joyful experience of it. We can know that in the fullness of our awakening into quantum realms, we won't be bored. Pure presence is ecstatic in nature. It is only our mental training that keeps us from experiencing the innate joy of being. When we don't feel joy, or when we experience boredom, we can know that this is only our mental desire to re-loop known patterns.

The level of illusion within the human perspective may also make us feel afraid to step into our ability to consciously create. It may be scary to have things manifest instantly in the moment we imagine them. Even if we have a very expanded perspective, we still experience and believe in a concreteness to this physical reality. It would be a big leap for our mind to conceptualize or understand instantaneous results to our desires, which is why we walk into our quantum creation abilities one step at a time.

The human mind, which we're used to operating from, cannot conceptualize the infinite nature of All That Is. Our perception of time is only as static as our minds are, which is why we must operate from the universal mind or higher mind in order to play in the quantum realms. When we let go of the mental desire to have a static reality, we open to perceive this higher level of reality.

When there is a moment of pause within the mind, especially when the mind is stunned for a moment and isn't grasping at anything, our mental matrix breaks open and we can see beyond the confines of time. In these moments, time seems to slow down or become more spaced out because we are entranced and viewing everything from a higher-frequency dimension—though to others viewing from the outside, events may appear to happen rapidly. Or we may see the entirety of a situation in one download. This is a sign that we have moved out of the linear idea of time into our higher-mind awareness, where everything does exist at once.

As we master our play with time, seeing the future becomes as comfortable and accessible to us as seeing the past. From this perspective the future reveals itself to us, and frequently, because it is normal in this realm. We begin to master the skill of consciously compressing time, and we can easily access points in our own individual timelines as if they are real in this moment now.

But it's helpful not to let our ability to see the future distract us from the present moment or make us feel like we need to be somewhere other than where we are. We don't need to see the future to feel safe. We don't need to know what the future brings when we are confident and trust the present moment.

And, if we are trying to see the future because we are afraid, we disregard the present moment and how powerful it is. Instead of trying to jump forward to see the future, we can sit in presence and call the future into our consciousness. When we do this, we can see everything much more clearly and create with trust and ease, without the lens of fear clouding our vision.

We are learning and experiencing how to be present on a timeline and simultaneously tap into our infinite nature. It is a paradox in human form: in the process of learning to see the future, we learn to simultaneously release it and not need to see it at all.

And, our choices and decisions are not as immutable as we may perceive them to be. As we move into universal consciousness, things are much less static and much more open. Time begins to shift and compress, and the speed of evolution amps up. Even painful moments, lessons or experiences will be shorter-lived and seem to speed by. We can know that in the ever-expanding infinite that is beyond mental comprehension, everything is in perfect order and happens in perfect timing. There is both time for everything, and a time for everything. Within the infinite now, we can consciously choose our timeline, and this gets easier with practice.

As we awaken and align more with our higher nature, we experience time in ways we never have before. We consciously enter the quantum field, where time is less linear and more like a multidimensional fabric.

In the quantum field, we get to choose from an expanded perception that is not constricted by unconscious patterns. Here we begin to see that we have infinite choices available to us, if only we can break through our own perceived limitations. We can disrupt the matrix—which is simply a web of patterns— and choose to step outside of it in order to truly create. We disrupt our own matrix of predetermined outcomes and actions by choosing from this higher perspective.

From the quantum field we cease to see problems, and instead only see infinite moments and experiences. There is nothing to hold onto, and nothing to fix. We recognize that everything we perceive now is actually an echo, a creation from the past, and that we are already flowing into our next creation. We even release things that are to come in our perceived futures, because we see that on some level they have already occurred. We appreciate all that is by allowing it to be what it is, without attachment. And then we play with it all: we move within our creations, we dance with them, and we continue to let new perceptions open to us.

We are learning pure presence, allowing ourselves to feel the power of each moment as it opens wide to show us the new opportunities that are now available. We are learning to know each moment as complete, in and of itself. We are being assisted into a quantum understanding of the flexibility of time. New codes coming into our physical reality—into our bodies and minds—make us more confident in the divine structure of time unfolding.

As we learn to play within the realms of quantum time and bring these time-bending abilities into our physical reality, we will become more able to consciously choose. And we will see that only when we are deeply present are we truly choosing and in full mastery of our choice.

Becoming the Observer

When we incarnate as humans, we move from the perception of ourselves as the infinite All into the perception of ourselves as a singular individual. This is the meaning behind what we call the fall of Adam: infinite consciousness moving from the eternal I AM space into the finite mind and awareness of self. The myth is that this was a fall or a mistake, when truly we wanted it this way. We wanted this more finite experience in order to have a new perspective. There is no self in the infinite space of I AM. Just as we can't look into our own eyes, we can't see a self from the space of eternal awareness.

To perceive ourselves as singular beings, we need to forget that we are the All. We travel into a denser reality and become convinced of our limitations, of the unfolding of time, and of our need to survive within the human game of birth and death. Our minds have assisted us in the game of separation, by creating and re-looping limited perception programs to convince us again and again that we are singular, finite beings.

In this density, the human mind has become very rigid in its limitations, and we have become used to this rigidity. This is similar to when one locks their jaw, and doesn't realize that they're unconsciously living with a tense jaw until it aches.

The human mind has been in this state for centuries, and it has been amplified to the point where it is ready to make a breakthrough. Like an orgasm, a release has to happen when something is amplified to such a state. And in this process of constriction and breakthrough, we get to experience spinning through the tight squeeze of a portal, followed by the weightless clarity of infinite openness.

When we enter into this spaciousness, into no-mind, we are in the realm of pure potential. There is a sense of awe at everything in existence. Here, we are in deep presence and allowance of all that is. From this expanded perception, life is a dance and everything is orchestrated in a much more harmonious and magical way than our mind can comprehend. In this space, we are the observer, not the thinker.

Being the observer is different than many may believe it to be. It is not a passive state; to be the observer does not mean to disengage or avoid participating in life, or to escape the drama momentarily. One who is being the observer is very involved with life, but from a perspective that sees the broader picture from higher dimensions.

When we are conscious only within the human plane of existence, we are trapped by its entanglements and rules. Becoming the observer means that we are aware but not attached, and that we know we are not bound to the rules of life. Instead, we allow, embrace, and dance with life—moving through energy beyond the realms of time and space. The observer sees with joyful fascination, makes broad sweeps and big moves, and can clarify all energies in an instant, bending and playing with time. When we become the observer, we are able to witness All That Is, and can then consciously choose our path. As gods, we are meant to continuously be the observer and to create from here.

This shift into the higher mind, or observer mind, requires that we become untethered and release the paradigms and belief systems that we have been holding onto for comfort, out of fear of lack. How could we ever lack anything when we are the All That Is? But these mental paradigms have been our unconscious structure throughout our lives, and so they can be difficult to release, no matter how freeing the higher realms are.

At times, moving into the observer mind will feel like going insane, because our minds are so attached to reality as we have been seeing it. At other times, this movement into higher mind will feel blissful, because it opens the capacity to create a new, much more pleasurable collective dream for our world.

From a higher-frequency perspective, the mental matrix is like a tightly woven fabric. Our mental matrix is created by repeating the programs of the ways that we've been trained to be and perceive. Our minds are often so locked up with programming and known information, that the downloads we wish to receive from higher frequencies can't come through. Our minds are tricky, jumping in to insert pre-written programs so quickly that we're sometimes not even aware that this is happening.

But when we are in the observer mind, the mental matrix clears and we are open to the All, and the streams of higher-frequency information become available to us. Our higher mind is completely efficient, simply existing in the deep presence of what is, channeling our higher self in each moment. Presence is the key: the more often we are present, the more we are able to create from, and anchor within, our higher mind.

This is why confusion is a good sign. When the mind already knows the path, we are engaged in closed-loop, circular and known programming; but when the mind is confused, there is more openness. Confusion is a sign that we are perceiving something outside of our programmed reality and are therefore open to more expansive information.

We often resist change because we have attachments to the status quo or to things that we believe are necessary for survival. We may feel afraid when we can't anchor internally to our old mental structures. We hold ourselves back from change because we don't know what to do or trust what is to come. But what is really happening is the mind doesn't know what to do based on what is already known and what has already been done. It may feel safer to re-loop old ways of being because they are familiar.

But the idea of wanting to resist change is a mental perception. Change is constant. Every moment is new. We are being asked to flow with these changes as we ascend.

However, we have to be gentle with ourselves for wanting to continue our routines and programs. These roots run deep, and our routines have helped us to feel safe. As we move forward as masters, though, it is our choice to move through these changes, release the patterns, and take the risk of letting go of the mental programming.

Many people are still loosening the tight hold that the mind has on them. In order to release these old patterns and evolve our consciousness, we need space to just be. It is helpful to give ourselves many moments throughout the day when our mental matrix is cleared—through practices of meditation and presence—to receive new information. As we do this, we build an inner remembrance of this space of timeless peace, beauty, and sovereignty.

Our Heart Leads

Though the mind plays a very important role in the process of coming into greater alignment, it is not meant to lead our experience in these higher-frequency dimensions. Our mind needs to be untangled from its re-looping patterns, and restored to its proper role as a support to the heart. Since it is a channel for the All That Is, our heart understands and holds the energy of the fifth dimension; so this is a good time for the heart to take the lead.

As we make this transition, we will discover that our heart has been guiding us the whole time, through everything we have experienced. It is as if the heart is the train conductor that nobody sees, and now it's ready to be more prominent. Everything that we know from the mind will be a tool that we can access to help us translate the powerful force of our heart. In all we do, the heart will guide the process.

Our human perception of the heart space is also elevating; we are becoming aware that the heart is the portal to our higher-self-awareness. In the same way that our minds are moving from small mind to the vastness of being the observer, our heart spaces are moving from the heaviness of emotionality into utter buoyancy, freedom and laughter. We become a channel of god consciousness, and we know that nothing matters because everything matters. What lightness and beautiful spaciousness lie within the heart, where we care about everything because we know it is a game. It is a vast shift, and we can see, feel, and sense evidence of this shift in ourselves and in the world.

At the initial stages of inhabiting our heart space, however, we may notice a lot of emotionality or fear emerging. This is a juncture of expansion, where we experience a volley between the heart and the mind: as the heart expands, our emotions become amplified to resist this change. We may feel a tightness in our hearts; this simply shows us a parameter or limit that the mind has placed around the heart space for safety. Our heart space is opening, and pushing our energetic walls back, which creates a feeling of tension. This may be confusing and make us want to close down again or do what is known, in order to retreat to a feeling of safety.

What is actually happening is that the mind is creating the very pain it is trying to protect us from: as the breakdown of old paradigms begins, the mind rushes in and attaches an emotional label to our experience—which is what activates our perception of pain. The pain doesn't exist until the mind rushes in. The human mind is programmed to problem-solve, but when we expand in the realms of the heart, we can't look at everything that breaks down and try to fix it. It is not meant to be fixed—it is breaking in order to open.

Therefore, all pain that we may feel within the heart space is simply a denser layer of reality breaking away to reveal our true, lighter frequencies. And contrary to what many people believe, the heart space is made to be strong. The true heart will never hurt, because the true heart exists outside the realms of duality and views all as love.

These shifts into the heart also don't have to hurt—in fact we don't even really need to pay attention to them. Pain comes from our perception of what is. But as gods, we know that everything is continuously flowing through the filter of our perception, and that we can command what is by changing our perception.

Instead of looking at things from a ground-level perspective, we need to expand out and look at the bigger picture. This is why many masters and meditation teachers teach non-attachment to our emotions—to let them be fleeting, like clouds in the sky. In becoming the observer, we begin to experience more and feel less, allowing our emotions to exist without attaching to them. We can zoom out and allow the breakdown of old paradigms to occur. We can allow and observe it all without dedicating our focus to it.

It can be scary to let go of our mental barriers, our perception of right and wrong, because when we do so, our worldview completely shifts. But we can relax in this process; we can move from being mind-centered to being heart-centered as slowly or as quickly as our comfort level permits. There is no rush; time is infinite, and we are infinite beings with infinite journeys of learning and soul growth.

The path of the heart master is one of immense bravery. It takes diligence and time to relearn and re-enter the strength and vastness of the heart space. Yet all things that emanate from the heart space are part of our purpose on this planet, and they ultimately come with an ease—once we allow this energy to flow through.

The heart speaks in a unique language and carries such a powerful frequency. We are still learning to listen to our heart and trust what it has to say to us. At times, we may not have the words for what we're experiencing, which reveals the purity of our experience. Universal nature does not require words, because from this expanded perspective it is not important to identify and encapsulate things.

As the heart space is increasingly activated, we grow stronger in our purpose, and what once seemed difficult will be easy. We can think of many examples of this in our life, where something was difficult at first but now is second nature. And truly, we could call living from our heart first nature, because it is our original nature. Our heart is who we are. Our heart's frequency is always emanating from us, no matter how many walls we put up, or how often we believe in this perceived reality and do everything we can to solidify it through the mind. The heart is always there as a portal to the infinite. Our nature is infinite, and that cannot be changed.

As we move the center of our awareness into the heart space, profound breakthroughs reveal themselves to us. While this may feel confusing or destabilizing, stepping into the unknown is really what the journey is about. Our journey is not about the actions that we take, but about learning to trust our highest input and exist in our highest frequency. As we do this, we will notice how it gets easier and easier; we will see that hearing, listening to, and trusting our heart is natural. We will learn to follow what our heart says, and then observe and feel everything that results from taking this step.

Pain and Suffering

Though it may not seem so at times, this life is a grand adventure. Being on our planet is simply a dense reality experience, and from a higher perspective nothing is ever wrong. We are not being tested, and therefore there is no such thing as failure. All is one, effortlessly spiraling into further and further expansion. But if everything is perfect and divinely guided, how do we make sense of experiences that are very difficult and cause a great amount of suffering—including those that seem to harm our minds and bodies?

On some level, we know that we did not come here to suffer. We came here to be, to know ourselves in a new way, and to experience our infinite nature within a reality of limitation—all in order to know that who we truly are is love. And yet from the limited perspective of the mind, we tend to place everything in two categories: good or bad. These categories are incomplete and fail to reflect the holistic truth of love. Love is quite literally All There Is—anything and everything that has ever been created or ever will be created. From expanded-frequency realms, even pain is seen holistically as an aspect of love.

In our human form, pain is the mind's interpretation that something is wrong. When we experience moments of pain, the mind sets out to create order from what it knows from previous experiences. The mind is seeking balance. But we will never find this balance when operating within the binary of good and bad; instead, we will continue to volley back and forth between these polarities. It is only when we can hold both perspectives at once that we can elevate to a higher frequency outside of the realms of duality. Balance and harmony are inherent in the realms of Oneness.

When we see something as painful or bad, this is because we are viewing it from our individual and limited perspective. Yet the very nature of suffering is an illusion, because it focuses on one perspective and not the fullness of all perspectives. From a sixth-dimensional awareness, we can see from all moments in time, and from within and outside of the experience. As highly conscious observers, we know that every occurrence is a divine moment within the multidimensional fabric of the All That Is.

Yet even as conscious creators, we will have times in life when we experience suffering and pain. Pain is an inherent part of the human experience, an inevitable aspect of the physical realms that we are playing within.

But pain can be of great service and a powerful teacher in our awakening, because it anchors the soul into the human experience. In painful moments, we are compelled to focus intently on what's happening, because we wish to rid ourselves of the pain. Our condensed emotions create a portal through which a greater amount of change can occur within a shorter period of time. Through pain, we have the potential to rapidly awaken and transcend the realms of time into the infinite now.

Pain can also help us collectively navigate into new experiences—because when many beings awaken to a place where undesired experiences are no longer tolerable, we pop through to the next realm and collectively awaken. This is often why there is a simultaneous and worldwide intensity or amplification of pain around certain behaviors or subjects. All at once, many people begin to feel pain or discomfort from experiences that used to be and feel normal. This is because as the planet awakens to higher-frequency realms, lower-frequency experiences become more acutely dense, and therefore more noticeable and uncomfortable.

All pain is a symptom of re-looping or not being fully present. In the moment that we perceive pain, we have the opportunity to become the observer. When we do this, our mind no longer blocks all that we are. We stop the cycle of recreating the pain long enough for a flood of light to rush through our body, and the body heals itself. This is immensely pleasurable; in fact, it's euphoric. Anytime we feel pain, we can know that it is a gateway to transcendence, if we can be fully present.

Through the feeling of contrast, pain activates and motivates us to gain clarity on what is no longer working for us. Being patient in our discomfort will allow us to learn to respond with awareness. We can then begin to choose from a place of internal peace, instead of continuing to need discomfort to motivate us. We can allow ourselves to breathe through these moments and feel the internal conflict without trying to fix it or fight it. And as we ascend, we will be more adept at being motivated by, and consciously choosing from, joy instead of pain.

There are three levels of moving through pain as we spiral upwards: acknowledging the pain and doing the shadow work; embracing the pain by recognizing it as holy; and dancing with the pain.

Our shadow work is a very literal process of discovering where we are casting our own "shadows," based on where we're blocking the eternal light that's beaming through us. Anything that stands between ourselves and Source casts a shadow. These are our pain bodies, our stuck energies, thoughts, and emotional states. As we consciously raise our frequency, we become more aware of different lower frequencies that filter our pure Source light.

Once we've done deep shadow work, we reach a zero point of clarity and equilibrium. If we don't then allow ourselves to elevate into play, we will continue to swing back and forth in duality and play the same game—getting stuck in the miserable limbo of continuous dramatic creation within lower-frequency realms. This is why shadow work needs to end, and why we must elevate to play once we reach neutrality.

Dancing with the pain is at the level of play. When we dance with the pain, we recognize that all occurrences are neutral and that, as creators, we can choose to play consciously in new ways. In this dance we find deep joy, and, ultimately, we transmute the previous paradigm of pain into love.

To consciously bring our awareness into infinite joy during moments of pain, our practice is to feel gratitude for the pain. This may seem to be the opposite of what we would want to do, but in appreciating anything, our perception of the finite falls away and the infinite rushes in. Beyond our mental perceptions, the infinite is always felt as joy to the system.

Our full acceptance of all our experiences is what unlocks the re-looping pattern and sets us free. But accepting exactly what is in the moment can be so difficult, as it causes us to release the stories upon which we have built our existence. Accepting everything can feel like losing our mind or losing our entire sense of self or core beliefs. It can even feel like a death, as the mind can't comprehend our existence without those beliefs. But if we allow it to, the discomfort we feel in these moments can push us through a portal into expansion.

Also, it is a fallacy that the old part of us must die in order to birth something new. The only thing that dies is the attachment to, and re-looping of, old patterns. Each new version of ourselves will not cost us the old version. Instead, the old becomes integrated in its fullness. All we are ever doing is expanding, and in expansion, we contain all we have ever been, and more.

Anxiety is another experience which we often misinterpret to be negative, but which we can learn to see in a new way. As the frequencies of the planet amplify, we become capable of perceiving and choosing from a vaster realm of possibilities. Many of us experience anxiety as the speed of inspiration increases; this is because we haven't yet practiced how to create as quickly as this inspiration comes to us—essentially at "light speed." In essence, anxiety is a sign of being overwhelmed by inspiration, and a desire to live our purpose.

When we are calling in who we desire to be in the future, we project ourselves away from our present moment, often believing that our present moment is out of alignment with our grander picture. But it is not. If we can release our need to pull the future toward us, and instead bring ourselves into present-time awareness and allow everything to be in this moment, we will always be led to our highest possible future, because we are existing in it now.

We can therefore remember that anxiety is anticipation and excitement for the newness of our creations. When we have feelings of anxiety, or any emotional reactions that move us away from our center, we can gently move into being the observer. From this space, most of the actions that we think we need to take will fall away, and new ones that we could not previously conceive appear. Being the observer and making all choices from this state is our true center of power. Even one moment simply existing as the observer is more powerful than any action we could take from a place of unconsciousness. Eventually, through practice, we move into a playful god consciousness and ask, "What is so absolutely joyful?" instead of, "What needs to be taken care of?"

We can always remember that moments of pain, anxiety, or discomfort—supposed blocks to the life that we desire—are simply part of the adventure that we are creating for ourselves. It is always an aspect of creation, and as such, we can feel proud of ourselves for all that we have created thus far. In these moments of pain, we can know that we are doing nothing wrong. We are not failing at fulfilling our purpose, nor are we failing anyone. In fact, we will have the capacity to provide so much more to others if we give ourselves the permission and space to feel unstable for a moment as we shift.

We can remember that we are in a period of massive awakening and transition, and so everything may feel uncomfortable at times. We are in motion, transmuting the old ways into the New. The best way to handle our transitions is to let ourselves have fun and explore the incredible nature of creation, with full acceptance of all our experiences.

Imagination, Choice, and Focus

Reality from the human perspective is simply a dream, an imaginative creation projected from our higher selves. Through our awakening, we are becoming lucid in the dream, so that we can play with mastery in our creations.

As the dreamers of our experience, we have infinite choice, and we get to choose our own adventure in this lifetime. Our ability to choose is our birthright. We are each gods, learning to create our unique worlds through the power of our imagination. Anything we can envision can be ours. In fact, our imagination is what creates our entire life experience.

But much of our dream is unconscious, and many of our imaginings are not our own. From the moment our soul comes into this human reality, we immediately begin receiving the imagined realities of others: ways of life that we have collectively (and mostly unconsciously) agreed upon. What seems "real" or "true" to us from our human perspective is simply something we have continuously imagined until it becomes a programmed reality. So often, we are simply dreaming what somebody has already dreamed or what we've been programmed to dream. We are walking a well-worn path.

Many programs have been repeated for centuries—not because they are objectively "true" or even beneficial for us, but because they have been promoted and repeated. And through our unconscious participation in them, we perpetuate the collective dream. Some of these programs serve us by helping us believe in this reality enough to play the game of being human. But some of these programs clearly don't serve us. Stories of lack, limitation, and separateness are all programs, imprinted stories that we have come to believe in these human realms, which no longer fit with the higher-frequency paradigms we are moving into.

Our imagination is our intentional dream. In a sense, imagination is true creation. Can we remember being a child and having our imagination feel just as real as the "reality" we were being taught about and living within? Through this awakening, we are being brought to a place where this is the case once more. Here, we imagine the world in its most pleasurable capacity. We exist in the realms of the unseen, beyond what our eyes have been taught to fixate on. And as we learn to see beyond our current paradigms, we know this new reality to be just as true as the reality that we believe we're seeing right now.

In order to consciously create a new reality, we need to release outdated, lower-frequency stories and intentionally dream a new dream. When we allow ourselves to imagine in a new way, we begin to see our world change to match our imagined creations.

In order to access the purest dreamscape, we need to first bring ourselves to our zero point.
Our zero point of creation is the vibrational place outside of duality. Here, we are the neutral observer. Here, we no longer

believe in the unconscious projections of the collective but instead know that we are the creators, projecting from the All. We know we are at our zero point when we feel the bliss of deep presence. This is complete surrender, where we allow the All That Is to project Source light through us in its fullness.

We can begin to access our zero point of creation by awakening to our unconscious programs. By consciously clearing these old programs and overlays, we start to find our true nature. We are no longer blinded by the parameters of the mind. We begin to know our limitless potential, without filters, and we can see the expansive level of choice available to us. From this perspective, we can move through this landscape of play more adeptly, and even in a way that is superhuman. This is creation on the level of gods.

Everything that we imagine is real within the higher-frequency realms. But as we get into the denser realms, we need to gather more energy around our imaginations to make them physical. We do this through our focus and the conscious choices we make.

The infinite play of the All That Is is formless and moves into form through focus. Our focus is what helps us choose our desired experience from the infinite and bring it into the present moment. This process is like taking the light of the sun and shining it through a magnifying glass; as the bringers of the light, we are the edge of the lens that focuses the All That Is and manifests it into matter. This focus creates more of whatever we're paying attention to, helping us solidify it in the physical. And in physical reality, we like so much to dive into one experience, and deeply discover that one experience.

There is an ease in creation that opens to us as we awaken to higher-frequency realms. We cease to see limitations, and we recognize that the power of our focus enables us to create beyond the confines of time and space. From our human perspective, events unfold along a timeline, and we are then at the mercy of this timeline, waiting for things to happen in the future. But from the expanded consciousness of knowing that everything is here and now, we can choose to focus on anything along that perceived timeline, because it is available to us in this moment; the more we focus on it, the more it anchors into and becomes created in the physical reality.

And so we begin to experience that everything is here and now, and we can bring something into physical truth through our study of it, our focus, and our passion to discover more about it. Simultaneously, we build an expanded view of all of the possibilities that are available to us. By allowing our passion to guide us, and observing, feeling, and becoming deeply in touch with the flow of life force energy that runs through us, we connect with the energy currents that run through all of life. And as we are able to tune in with all energies, will we be able to redirect them.

Our focus is much more powerful than we may think. Indeed, focusing is choosing. We're almost lazy with where we place our attention, because we don't realize that it actually matters. As a result, we will often bring something back that we want to go away, simply due to the power of our focus. As we become more conscious within these expanded realms, we see that we create through every thought and every place where we direct our gaze. We create more of what we focus on; so when we want something to stop, we simply stop giving it attention.

Because we are still coming into awakened consciousness within higher-frequency realms, our expansive ability to focus and choose often feels frightening or overwhelming. We may have so many emerging ideas, burgeoning excitements, and desires that we wish to fulfill and bring into fruition in the physical realms. With this flood of expansive inspiration, we may not know what to choose, or we may hold ourselves back from making choices due to fear. But we only feel this reticence when we operate from our minds.

There is a startling difference between the way our minds function in the dense realms, and the ease, weightlessness, and freedom in eternal creation. When we enter that spaciousness after living from the mind, it may feel uncomfortably open. And yet this openness is the precipice of god consciousness. We are standing at the edge of creation, looking out at the potential and saying, "Yes I'd like to put my attention there." Our play on the quantum level is to point at what we like the most and bring these things into existence.

Knowing that we create through our focus may feel daunting to some of us, because we may feel our ability to focus is haphazard at best. But this is a skill that we can develop, and it will become second nature as we move away from fear-motivated living into a more expansive perspective.

As we practice focus, we also learn energetic integrity. When we use the word 'integrity' in relation to a physical object or structure, we mean that it is well built; if we say that a boat has integrity, we mean it doesn't have holes and it's not going to sink. If we have energetic integrity, it is similar; it means we are more discerning with what we focus on and what we let in. We love ourselves enough to turn away from what is not in alignment, in favor of what feels fun and resonant. Essentially, we learn to say, "This boat only carries these things."

Focus is a step in opening to the infinite. We learn how to gently lift our focus from one thing and place it on another. As we practice consciously focusing, we bring in a continuously broader perspective to play with, and simultaneously learn to align our energy with our desires.

Therefore, it is necessary to become more conscious of our desires and actively say yes to them. When we don't say what we want, we continue to get whatever just naturally flows in, like some very pretty moths and some not-so-fun moths drawn to the light of our personal universal consciousness. To draw in something specific, we need to choose it and allow it into our existence.

Transition from focus: Sometimes we avoid choosing because we believe that saying yes to one option means saying no to another thing. We're often afraid of closing doors because we don't want our choice to eliminate potential options. We fear the perceived permanence of a choice. But choosing is not the same thing as limiting. There is actually infinite expression within a tighter focus. In being more discerning, we only focus on what we desire more of, and whatever we're focusing on expands.

As we're learning to create and focus on our chosen viewpoint, we will encounter what we perceive to be distractions. But from a holistic perspective, there is actually no such thing as a distraction. Everything we meet along our journey is resonant with us in some way. This means that what we see as a distraction is either an opportunity for love and integration, or an invitation for expansion into more play.

"Distractions" therefore come to us for two reasons: either we are shaking off a pattern and learning deeper focus, or we mistakenly perceive something as a distraction that is actually part of our journey—and our minds don't yet comprehend how it fits into the overall picture of our intended creation.

The best way to discover whether something is a pattern we are shaking off or an opportunity for expansion and play is to engage and be present with it. If something is an old paradigm that we're releasing, such as self-hate or fear, our presence with it will make it whole and integrated. And if something is intended for our expansion and play, our presence with it will help us relax and consciously play with it.

As we step into this expanded level of choice, we may wonder if we can trust ourselves to know which direction to choose. How can we know what to choose if we've never experienced it before? How can we know what will bring us joy? How can we know that we won't miss out on something by choosing one thing over another?

We can't know these answers in the way we have before— which was through the mind, empirical evidence, and "logic." But we can know through our subtle senses, which are always guiding us into alignment with our divine blueprint. We can begin to sense and trust our own internal compass, feel the wind of inspiration, and move with it towards the creation of all that we desire. And so instead of asking, "How can I know?" or "What should I do?" we can begin to ask, "How can I better find my internal sense of knowing and self-trust, to know the answer to these questions myself?"

In the realms of the true creators, we're each receiving our own divine guidance. We previously externalized our power—and thus our ability to choose—because we believed that other people knew more than we did. We are now being called to embody more self-trust than ever before, which means we intentionally get to play with making choices, instead of giving our power of choice to others or hoping someone will decide for us. We learn to command our lives by embracing our desires and actively choosing them.

Self-trust means learning how to be in alignment with our inner truth. It means learning how to love all that we are, without exception. Therefore, trusting in ourselves is really trusting in our eternal nature. As we go into new experiences that our minds can't preconceive or understand, we are trusting that we are held and safe by the All. This is why we are called to practice stillness within the mind and move into the heart. When we tune into those still moments between actions, we feel our infinite nature, and the truth of who we are is revealed. We find the quietness of the observer and move beyond the frantic need to find answers.

It can be hard to be within the stillness of creation, and to relax and do what feels like nothing, when we're so used to constant action on the physical level. In fact, many may wonder how stillness and creation can coexist. Isn't creation a kind of activity? But in stillness we discover the expanded truth available to us: that the Void is creation itself. When we are conscious within the Void, we become aware that we are simply choosing the creation we would like to bring forth from the limitless All.

As we learn to relax, we see that any action we feel inspired to take comes naturally. We learn to flow with actions as they emerge, rather than obstructing or blocking them. We spend more time in the infinite bliss of the moments between moments, in the breath between thoughts. And as we connect these moments and make them more frequent, they will begin to create the new reality that we are already gravitating toward. As we do this we begin to move with mastery through life.

And we can remember to be playful in the process. Being in command of our choice is not only about taking full responsibility for ourselves. It is also about joyfully embracing our power to choose every moment of our lives as creators. We don't focus on the heaviness of responsibility, but on the freedom and lightness that come from allowing ourselves to attune to our power as conscious creators in every moment. We recognize endless choices and believe that they are all available to all of us, without limit. We can navigate our choices by paying more attention to what lights us up than to what feels uncomfortable. And when something doesn't feel good, that's great information; we can now turn toward what is desired and move in that direction.

Also, when we consciously choose from a higher-frequency perspective, we are firmly rooted in knowing that there is no right and wrong. To awaken does not mean to become good; it means to play with more consciousness. If we continue to play the game of believing in right and wrong, we will continue to make our decisions out of fear of making the wrong choice. But when we choose from a higher perspective, we are motivated by the joy of choosing and a desire to create. We know that all aspects of creation are neutral until we add our energetic propulsion to them. Things don't have to be bad for us to let go of them; instead, we can choose based on our preferences and a desire to align with our truth. In this new awareness, we move beyond ideas of right and wrong into the expanded perspective of eternity and oneness.

We also don't need to know all of the ramifications of every choice that we're ever going to make—and in fact, we can't. We've got to play within the timeline along the way and allow the energy of our creations to manifest as we arrive.

Even with focus, creation is not linear. Creation is allowing things to unfold and being in the flow state of expansion with joy, and ease. More and more, we're learning how to play, how to enjoy life, how to not be linear and yet still understand and operate with focused intention to consciously create.

We are meant to feel confident in choosing. Our power is not centered on what we choose, but in the fact that we are the chooser, the creator. Choosing is what we do. Our purpose is not to make the right choice, but to choose, period. Our power is in allowing ourselves to choose and not feel trapped by our choice or afraid that we've made the "wrong" one—for the truth is, we can't make a wrong choice. There is no one path for any one person, but rather infinite choices of avenues to take.

This life is for our exploration and continual learning. As we anchor into our self-trust and play with our imaginative creations, we awaken to more of the truth of who we are. We begin to know ourselves as gods—in fact, we begin to let go of the dream that we were ever not this. We begin to trust ourselves on a new level—not from the place of our finite ego, but from our ability to hold the fullness of the All, and to choose from this space. And as we recognize this is all a dream and see from a higher perspective, we know that everything is always in divine order. Our collective expansion into higher frequencies is simply a matter of many people dreaming a new dream together.

Divine Blueprint

Each of our lives are so meaningful. Our individual existences are important, and our unique frequencies are an essential aspect of this reality. We are created, have created ourselves, and are continuously creating ourselves in harmony with All That Is. We are interconnected, woven into the spectrum of these realities, divine and intentional.

In other words, we are all absolutely perfect. As unique embodiments of divine source, we are all deserving of a great wealth of unconditional love. There is nothing we ever need to change, even in the moments in which we feel out of alignment. This is simply a fun game to play—to continuously grow and shift and transform, and to know through experience that we are powerful creators. There is no being on the planet who is not of absolute importance, and this realm would be infinitely changed without our existence within it.

As powerful gods, we fully create all aspects of our own human existence: our lives, our trajectories, and all our states of being. Not only are we creating our outer world; we are also playing with the creation of ourselves down to our very bones. Everything about each one of us is malleable and shiftable; there is no part of ourselves that cannot be utterly transformed.

And yet with all of this multidimensional awareness, we are still within the human perspective. It can be tricky to understand how to navigate our ability to choose. Additionally, we are in a time of great change; there is an understandable and prevalent desire to have an anchor as we move through these massive shifts. How do we choose from infinite choices, and still feel stable?

It can be helpful to know that while we are capable of an incredible amount of change, there are aspects of each human which are meant to be more static and consistent. On a physical level, this is our DNA, but that concept falls short of the expanded truth of the higher realms. From a higher perspective, it is our divine crystalline structure, our human template or blueprint. Each of us created these templates for ourselves before we incarnated ("before" meaning that it was placed on the timeline previous to our human existence, even though there is no linear time within the All). These templates are meant to serve us in our human capacity and help us to align to the life we chose for ourselves "prior" to incarnation.

Our divine blueprint is what guides us to fulfill our life's purpose. Each of us has a gift to bring into the world. We are all born to do something great, to serve in our highest capacity by bringing the fullness of ourselves through into this physical plane. We feel an inner calling, a thirst that is only quenched through active participation in our specific vibratory field. This inner calling is our life's purpose.

The idea of a life purpose often translates within our human sphere to a specific form of work or action-taking, a job or a duty to fulfill. But our divine purpose is not about what we do. Our real life's purpose is to emanate our specific energy signature, our frequency. Living our purpose means tuning in more accurately to our unique, specific energetic signature and streaming this into the physical realms. Our individual human templates are what guide us toward the energetic frequency of who we are and what we are meant to emanate and create in this lifetime. It is all written within us.

Yet even though we have this template written within ourselves, we experience amnesia when we enter these denser human realms. This is an essential part of the game of being a human: we don't remember the fullness of who we are, and we don't know why we're here or what we created for ourselves. So how do we know what to do with our lives? How do we know what is written within our template?

Our answer to this question is simple: we do whatever we want. This is not an offhand comment, but direct guidance. We do what we want to do. We follow our desires. These desires guide us to be who we intended ourselves to be, and they activate us along the journey of reawakening to the fullness of our true selves.

Each person is imbued with unique desires because they are part of our specific, individual human template. Our desires come directly from Source, channeled through the perfection of our energetic frequency into this reality. Desires are clues for us. They show us evidence of our blueprint and move us along from one juncture in our fabric of time to the next. Our desires are holy, guiding us in our individual journeys to the truth of our divinity. And each emerging desire is a sign of an activation within our blueprint.

We have different levels of desires that emerge from within ourselves; some are more in alignment with our true self, directly encoded within our template, while others are more surface-level, or ego-guided desires.

Our surface-level desires emerge from the mind and are driven by the motivation to keep us safe in various ways. We often experience them as "needs," because we feel scarcity, or we fear that they won't be fulfilled. We have become accustomed to satisfying these desires in order to operate within the physical realms. And yet these desires are like mirages on distant planes; they point us to a core desire, but they don't fully satisfy us. Now as we awaken and can see multidimensionally, we know that our human needs will absolutely be taken care of. As we ease into the calm of knowing that we are held and cared for by the All That Is, we begin to see our core desires emerging from our divine template.

Core desires are born of the truth of who we are; they emerge directly from our divine blueprint. Our blueprint is the highest-frequency expression of ourselves; therefore, whenever we choose our highest vibrational expression, we are naturally choosing our blueprint.

We know that something is a core desire, a pure desire born from our blueprint, because it lights up our entire body with joy. And in fact, our purpose as creators is to bring more light from the Void into the physical realms. Thus, when we create through our sacred desires, we feel lit up. We feel a rush of joy, anticipation, and delicious happiness when we receive an idea or an inspiration that is going to take us down the path of our internal blueprint. Curiosity and excitement are signs that a desire is emerging directly from our human template and pointing us to something we were born to create.

Knowing that not all desires are core desires should not stop us from following them. Sometimes we don't even know what will light us up because we have blocked our desires for so long. We've been taught to block the light, to not trust our own illumination. As we learn to make choices on a conscious mastery level, we may feel a desire without our whole body lighting up—initially—until we actually choose it and go along that path a little bit. This is why it's a good idea to follow our desires, regardless of whether we know they're core desires or not.

As we begin to play more consciously, we get used to making choices from a desire to expand and experience, rather than a desire to keep ourselves safe. We become more and more comfortable with choosing, and we allow the joy of our desires to flow through us and light our path.

Desires are often terrifying from the human perspective, because they carry such a powerful energy. Indeed, an emerging desire carries the energy of the fullness of who we are—and the fullness of who we are is Source light, streaming directly into this physical plane. This light was too overpowering in times past.

We also may fear our desires, because original sin programming has taught us that we are inherently fallible. We are taught that there is such a thing as right and wrong, and we worry that our desires will lead us down the "wrong" path. But our desires are the path. And in fact, there isn't a right path, or a specific path, for any of us. In the quantum now, we are engaging with the journey of play. It is not a linear journey, but an exploration within the fabric of time.

Our purpose here on Earth is to expand, not to achieve some idea of perfection. Our ideas of perfection are actually a fracturing of self, a misunderstanding of the greater truth that we are already the All That Is. The idea of perfection is based on the old-paradigm belief of right and wrong. But there is no action that is not perfect within the higher-consciousness realms. Here we know that we are masters, and that all creation throughout all timelines is inherently "good," because there is no opposite to that.

Instead of attempting to be perfect in our choices, we follow what brings us the most joy, because joy is in our highest frequency—which is the frequency of our blueprint. And thus, we get closer to our core desires when we allow ourselves to be "imperfect" and play with life. In following the desires that we feel will bring us the most joy, we learn and naturally get closer to the truth of who we are and the blueprint that we set out for ourselves.

Open and Specific Templates

At our core, our purpose is so simple: to exist, and to stream our individual frequency signature into the fabric of this time and space playground.

We have all built our individual templates to work in harmony with the All, and also to create in ways that are unique to each individual. Within our individual human template structures, some have more specific codes and highly curated callings, while some are truly here for the Earth experience and to play broadly. Those of us who have specific encoded templates and many specific destination points to meet chose these moments and activation points in our lives because we are wayshowers; we are here to activate and show the way for a particular plan that is unfolding.

How can we know if we have a more open template or a more specific template? This is not something we need to worry about, because what is written for us will be; it is a truth of harmony that is clear within the higher-frequency realms. Those who are built to choose within a specific template will choose it, and those who are given unlimited choice will naturally play with that openness.

It can be helpful to know that those with specific templates experience callings which surface as deeply compelling desires. People with a more specific inner structure are also often given visions or premonitions of what their future will look like, as a way to help them choose it again.

For those of us who do have more specific templates and feel a deep desire to fulfill a particular path, it may weigh heavily on us to think we could somehow miss a specific juncture point and not fulfill our callings. And it is true that at times, we may create a delay in meeting certain checkpoints or activation points within our blueprint—because the thrill of being human and re-looping experiences is so compelling. But we can take comfort in knowing that what is written for us is inevitable.

Sometimes we have a misconception that we will miss something permanently, and a door will forever be closed to us. If this strikes a fear in us, it is because we do not yet perceive the truth of our eternal nature. Our desires exist on a level of pure frequency, and therefore are not tied to any specific action. And so, yes, there can be missed opportunities, missed connections, missed moments of engaging with something or someone in particular. But this does not mean we will actually miss anything from an energetic frequency perspective.

Many of us with specific templates are given visions of our future, to guide us toward what we previously have chosen for ourselves. When we receive a vision of our future, it is because it is absolute—meaning that based on our vibratory set-point or resonance, it is an inevitable checkpoint in our life. With that being said, we can determine how long it takes to get there; we can decide how many pit stops we take along the way. But we will get there.

In creating our templates, some of us knew that we would want to feel the freedom of choice but never lose sight of the deep desire or purpose that we set out for ourselves in this lifetime. And so we built ourselves to be very sensitive, so that it would be too uncomfortable for us to choose outside of our template and not fulfill our sacred callings.

As masters, we each have so much that we desire and are calling in to create. When we relax in knowing that everything we desire is guaranteed, we will be less conflicted in our desires, and able to manifest them more easily.

Starseeds and Past Lives

For those who are newer to this human experience—often called starseeds—our purpose is to carry the codes of a higher-frequency star system or collective within our template. We do this in order to show the beings of the Earth what we are all evolving into, and to help open up channels for the Earth to move into higher frequencies. By being a channel for these frequencies, we ignite people's memories of unity consciousness, infinite love, and our potential to exist in these states consciously.

For starseeds, our energetic signature is encoded with the frequencies of where we're from—where our soul was "seeded" or created—as well as with the frequencies of many other star systems where we have existed and learned. We are always connected to these frequencies, and by existing on Earth, we create a direct channel from that cosmic energy to this incarnation.

Since starseeds are newer to the human experience, we often have intense experiences built within our blueprint immediately upon birth or early in life. We give ourselves these experiences to help us have compassion and understanding for the perception of pain that others on this planet have—which is more deeply embedded in them from lifetimes of Earth experiences. Newer souls are more aware that we're dreaming of and creating this experience, so we create intense experiences for ourselves in order to feel pain and make this Earth experience feel more real.

But even though we planned to have these experiences, newer souls often find pain to be confusing, because it is unfamiliar. Pain is a much denser frequency than what we're used to, because our soul memory is so close to light frequencies where pain exists only as a concept. For souls newer to this human experience, being in the Earth reality is like being in water and needing to swallow rocks in order to stay within this density. How uncomfortable this feels! But there are many people who are familiar with this heavier density because they have played within the human realms throughout time. Those who are more familiar with Earth lives recognize that it is normal to be in pain in many different ways. As starseeds learn to transmute the pain of their human experiences, they gain the valuable experience of multidimensionality, becoming more grounded and able to adeptly play within the Earth realms while still bringing their starseed frequency.

Those who have lived many Earth lives bring valuable gifts to this awakening time as well, because they have learned so much through these experiences that can serve in this present life. They bring the many lessons, tools, and keys they have gathered across lifetimes of experiences to assist in the ascension process of us all.

At times, memories from past lives come to us. (and "past" simply refers to where something occurred within the fabric of time.) When we're shown visions of soul memories from past lives, we're being guided to become aware of, access, and unlock something that we have already learned and mastered, something that we're meant to work with in our present life.

This is true of everything that comes into our awareness. When something comes across our path, especially when it lights up for us or lights us up, it is meant for us at that time. Everything that illuminates us is for our personal enlightenment. It is our divine calling being activated, and we are holding the frequency needed to bring it into our awareness at that point in our personal timeline. It wouldn't come to us if it wasn't the right time, or if we weren't ready.

However, there are people who spend endless amounts of time diving into past lives. This is a bit like getting stuck in shadow work, which has the effect of re-looping and recreating continuously. Even if we were shown everything we've experienced in all of our lifetimes, and every possibility that could exist, it would likely be of little use to us in this lifetime. The experience that we're having here and now needs to have our focus. This human life is about exploring a specific trajectory, which is the blueprint that we created for ourselves.

Opening to Our Desires

As we're learning how to actively choose, we'll inevitably notice a backlog of old desires come up, wanting to be fulfilled. This is because in our unconscious states, we've been choosing outside of our core desires—instead satisfying our ego and our human desire for safety through secondary or tertiary desires. We may feel overwhelmed by creative impulses and desires that seem to be insatiable as we awaken to our truth.

Many of us have been stuck for a long time—possibly our whole lives. Therefore, any movement we make is going to provide both relief and discomfort. The relief can be a visceral feeling of finally freeing ourselves from self-imposed restrictions. Simultaneously, discomfort in the form of pain or anger could arise, because we have disregarded our desires for so long. Discomfort is not necessarily a sign that we're doing something wrong; in fact, it can show us that we're creating movement where we have held back for a very long time. Like a limb that has its blood circulation cut off for a moment and wakes up again, the core of who we are is emerging, and this powerful emergence may register as discomfort in our body.

Most of us have downplayed our longings because we want to be present and not live in some unsatisfied idea of the future. We've been taught that longing means yearning for something that is unfulfilled. But a better way to interpret longing is as a signpost for an awakening desire, a desire that is reaching out and saying, "I am a part of you, and I am calling you toward your truth."

So often, we limit ourselves because we do not trust our desires. In our expansion, we come to realize that allowing our desires to flow through us is not only for our own fulfillment. Our awakening is not only for ourselves, it is our contribution to the entirety of existence. Each of us is an essential aspect of the All. Our inherent desires are our gifts to share with the world. They need to come out, and they need to be shared— channeled through our voices, our bodies, our creations—and shine for all to witness. This is our service to each other.

This energy that desires to move through each of us is so powerful. It can almost be incapacitating to feel the ecstasy of it moving through our human system—especially if we have previously held back. And as we allow the desires from within our template to emerge, more will come through. This process can be overwhelming.

To ease the overwhelm, we can open up to the flow of our desires gently, by letting ourselves make small shifts and do minor things differently. This can be anything: going to a different grocery store, writing in a journal, or talking to someone we don't know. When we get an impulse, instead of stopping ourselves, we act on it and release the bottleneck of creative power within us. As we attune to our divine template, we don't have to seek out our backlogged desires; we discover them simply because we are not blocking them. There is a tremendous amount of inner strength—true strength—that comes from allowing this flow.

Flowing with the divine timing of our blueprint feels ecstatic. When we are truly in the flow of our purpose, we feel it not just in our mind but also throughout our body. We can know that we are centered in our purpose through this ecstatic vibration.

Spontaneity and Destruction

Spontaneity is incredibly helpful in shaking off our conditioning. In fact, it is a core aspect of the nature of creation: it is the spark. Some people resist spontaneity because they perceive it to be unruly and out of control—and thus inherently destructive. But when we truly understand spontaneity, we know that it is incredibly loving.

True spontaneity is actually just pure presence, the natural result of the stream of love we channel from universal consciousness. Being spontaneous is recognizing the present moment and allowing ourselves to be unfiltered and flow within it. This only feels "spontaneous" to the mind, because our mind is so programmed to hold attachments and focus outside of the present moment. Spiritual awakenings, kundalini rising, instantaneous openings of the energy portals within our bodies, and even "love at first sight"—which is an awakening to a soul-level recognition—are all considered to be spontaneous. They are also all incredibly divine events.

Even what we perceive as destruction is really just a moment in an ever-flowing cycle. In this time-based density realm, all things are breaking down, reforming, breaking down and forming again.

On a physical level, destruction can look scary and even may seem to hurt people. But perceived from higher-frequency realms, destruction is simply the breakdown of something that was not meant to hold its stability in the present moment. And as we come into greater alignment with the higher-frequency realms, many structures of the lower-frequency realms will fall apart. If something breaks down while we are in a high level of presence, it was never meant to be sustained.

It's hard for humans to believe that destruction is neutral, or even good and positive, because our perception is limited in this time-based reality. Instead of perceiving everything as now, we become aware of things as they unfold across the fabric of time, moment to moment. We don't see the full picture all at once, but rather catch things in process: a moment of breakdown, a moment of rebuilding, a moment of creation. We see each moment as isolated in order to play with the unfolding. We created this game of being human so that we could have a myriad of experiences and believe in them while we're experiencing them.

As we ascend to higher frequencies, we see more holistically. We see that moments are not isolated, and we become aware of the beauty of them all working together. We see how perfect every single seemingly isolated experience is as a part of the whole. We know that in every moment of perceived destruction there is also simultaneous creation, and that everything is flowing and cycling perfectly—harmoniously orchestrated within the All beyond our human perception.

This incredible Earth can teach us a lot about destruction being a beautiful experience. The earth is literally made of destruction: it is formed from the breakdown of matter that becomes the building blocks of something new. Without destruction, nothing would ever change or move. We tend to look at destruction in terms of humans doing things to each other from a place of unconsciousness, and this is scary from our limited perception. But nothing can ever truly die. It is all a part of a continuous cycle.

In higher consciousness, polarized experiences are neutralized, and there is balance. Nothing can disturb these high frequency levels, because they are not opposed to anything. From here we flow playfully and with ease, creating in alignment with our divine human template.

Relationships in Universal Love

As we move into our mastery and operate within quantum realms, the way we connect with other beings inherently changes. We expand our understanding of what relationships are, and what it means to be interconnected and also unique and sovereign beings. Collectively, we're moving from operating in human love into the expression of a more divine, universal love.

We can think of universal love as the fullness of the spectrum of light that we can bring forth from the Void, while our human expression of love has been just one or two colors from this spectrum. Universal love is unconditional; it is love without the parameters and boundaries created by dualistic paradigms. As we expand into universal love consciousness, the way we operate and exist in the world is increasingly guided by our own internal blueprint, and less by attachment to the programs we have previously been creating from.

There are many limitations in human love. In human love, we are guided by ego and survival, and we connect with each other from the perception that we are merely physical beings, motivated by basic needs. But divine love is expansive and whole. Here we understand that we are all one, and that we are playing as individual expressions while in human form. Our connections with each other are an expression of this higher-frequency love, wherein we mutually honor each other's inherent divinity.

When we connect to each other in the space of universal love, each expanded being has so much more access to the fullness of all that we are; our connections become explosive god creations, where one amplified energy connects with another. This is the meaning behind the bible verse, "When two or more are gathered together in my name, there I am in the midst of them." Coming together at this level is an incredibly powerful co-creation on the level of gods. It is pure play.

From a physical perspective though, universal love can seem confusing. We come into this human experience as babies, completely physically helpless beings. We learn that to be loved is to be kept safe and cared for by another, and that to love someone is to provide for them in all ways, including physically—by feeding, sheltering, and protecting them.

And indeed, this is the beginning of the game. From the very beginning, the playing field is set up to create mental parameters that teach each individual the rules of this physical sphere. We make it absolutely apparent upon birth that matter is real; that one must eat to survive; and that to feel psychologically healthy, one must be loved and cared for and in turn care for others.

It can be very difficult, then, to remember our infinite nature—to know that we are eternal and can never truly be harmed or destroyed. There are truths within the physical world that absolutely do exist: human bodies need to be fed; sleep needs to occur; and if we go underwater for ten minutes we will likely drown! But when we trust in each other's inherent god-selves, we trust in the expanded consciousness aspect of each individual within this human realm. And we know that even if we are unable to provide for, care for, or shelter those we love, we can trust that every individual is infinite, and everything is always in perfect order.

This does not rule out the reality that one can suffer and even go to the lengths of dying in this physical plane. Universal love includes all of this and knows that nothing is ever wrong. Universal love operates on a higher perspective, from the knowledge that while we are in this human playing field, certain allowances do need to be made in order to play the game and move within the laws of each realm.

Existing in this higher love does not mean that we deny care for another being on the human level or intentionally create suffering. In fact, the opposite is true: when we are in the frequency of universal love, we desire to bring our full and unrestrained love and care to each other. In fact, we are able to bring more love, because we are not bound by people-pleasing or egoic love—which are based on the idea of depleting ourselves to give to another. Instead, we love ourselves deeply and give to others from the space of this love.

In this higher consciousness, we come to know that others are allowed to experience, believe, and know absolutely anything they desire—even if it causes them suffering on a human level. From this perspective, we understand that all beings choose their life's journey and create their own blueprint to guide themselves through it. We honor that each person comes into this life to have an infinite array of experiences while in human form—which includes suffering as well as immense joy.

Universal love also operates within the knowing that we are all masters with the potential to consciously embody our mastery in this lifetime. Human love has always been conditional, creating parameters around what actions are needed in order to receive or give love, and punishing each other for moving outside of these parameters. But this is not the case with universal love. Universal love honors and trusts the infinite nature of each individual and knows that each person has divine choice. From universal love, we know that it is each individual's choice to open to their divinity or keep it shut off from themselves. If they shut themselves off from the frequency of universal love—which inherently causes suffering—then that is a beautiful experience they are choosing to have, and universal love will never interfere with that.

Universal love may sound overwhelming, or even inaccessible. Yet on some level, we know this is what is possible and what we truly desire to feel in all our connections. This power is the very reason that we are compelled to connect with each other. Even in our human realms, we can access and embody universal love. All we need to do is awaken. This level of creation requires each of us to be in vibrational alignment with our higher self—which operates from the consciousness of universal love—and then stream this expanded consciousness into our human experience.

Co-creation With Others

There are many games we can play and experiences we can co-create in relationship with others. Playing with each other from an elevated place of love is a joyful experience. But at times, our connections may create a great deal of confusion and a sense of losing ourselves in each other. For this reason, it can be deeply empowering to understand how we interact and share our realities with one another, so that we can navigate towards more loving and empowering co-creations together.

We can imagine each individual's consciousness as if it is within a bubble. As we move through life, we project our reality from within ourselves onto the inner walls of the bubble surrounding us in order to create our worlds. Each being is projecting their own perception of the world into their reality, and all projections are true and real to each being.

When we connect with another person, we share a projection wall, like the edges of two bubbles meeting. If someone comes into our sphere, or if we are in their sphere—and this can be energetically and not just physically—we are mutually projecting a similar reality that is mirrored on our shared walls. Our collective reality is the shared result of our individual creations. It is our co-creative dream.

Playing with others is an exercise in balance. How much can we let into our worldview from another person while being centered in ourselves and our personal truth? At times, we pay so much attention to the reflections outside of ourselves that we lose our own experience, and thus our own joy. This is an externalization of our power. But we are sovereign beings who create the dream that we walk within, even if we are not always conscious of it. In our awakening, we are being called to meditate and feel our own energy, to not look outside ourselves for answers but simply exist in the knowing that our happiness comes from within.

In our awakening, we become more conscious of the dream we are creating for ourselves and of our own projection of reality.

This is because we experience a dimensional shift and begin to view life from the perspective of universal love. In this state, an elevated and expanded capacity for self-love also emerges. The memory and knowledge of who we are as divine beings begins to return to us, and we begin to feel this divinity within. From self-love, we allow ourselves the freedom to be unique and exactly as we are. When we return to ourselves in this way, we can make more conscious choices about what we want to project and the experiences we want to create with each other.

Through this process of coming into greater self-love and sovereignty, many patterns of disempowerment will arise and show themselves to us. These include codependency, dynamics of control, and people-pleasing. With greater self-love, manipulative and transactional love also fall away. Every program we are running that externalizes our power will become apparent and serve as a call for us to heal and return to ourselves.

Many of us are running a pattern of codependency, wherein we attempt to fill the hole in our heart with another person. But we come to see that it hurts our heart when we try to make someone else the center of our focus; when we do this, we give them the power to our happiness and feelings of safety. This is a distortion. Others do not have the authority to be the creators of our reality—we are the creators, and therefore we are at the center of our creation. We learn that we have to fill our heart first with our own self-worth, self-love, and joy for being alive, instead of attempting to source these from other people.

Many of us come to believe that another person's opinion matters so much that we let it shake our foundation. Yet in order to expand beyond the limits of egoic love into universal love, we can't place importance on what others think or believe about us. Human emotions are volatile; if our focus is on assuaging or calming others, we will always be jumping back and forth, and we will always lose our power in the process. With greater self-love, we are no longer concerned about hurting someone's feelings to the point that we end up hurting ourselves, and we stop taking responsibility for others' emotional states. We don't need to prove our magic, our worth, or the truth of who we are to anyone.

We may wish to be seen and accepted by other people, but it is helpful to know that nobody can see us or recognize us until we see ourselves. When we are able to love someone—regardless of their feelings toward us—we will feel free. We will be able to move through every situation with a deep compassion and love for ourselves, and we will naturally draw in people who also want to meet us in this energy.

If we could truly understand the effect that our unique individual vibration has on the world, we would never be worried about how others perceive us. We would always feel loved. The brightness of each soul currently inhabiting this human creation is what makes it whole. Our unique light is more brilliant than we could ever imagine, and each of us is an integral part of this entire fabric of reality. We each have a specific and integral role in the unfolding of each other's life paths as well.

At times, we may also wish to slow our expansion or not bring forth our personal creations because we worry that if we ask for what we want, or if we live our happiest life, it could somehow hurt those around us. We think, "Why should I have what I want? What makes me special, to be worthy of this?"

This comes from a belief in limitation in the Universe. In this belief, we actually dishonor each other's mastery and ability to choose. Loving others means that we recognize we are all masters, and we accept and honor each other's choices. If we did believe in everyone's inherent mastery, what would be the most loving thing we could teach them about how to wield that mastery? Most likely we would also want them to be unlimited and to ask for anything they want—because they deserve it. The more we do this for ourselves, the more we carve a path for others to do so as well.

As humans who live with so much lack mentality, it can be difficult for us to agree that there are infinite possibilities for everyone. It may be uncomfortable for some people to allow themselves unconditional joy in a world that says this is not possible; this idea is often the opposite of what we've been programmed to believe. We are taught that suffering is normal, and that to be joyful means that we're "not paying attention." But the more we sift through these programs of suffering and move in the direction of joy and play, the more we know that not only is unconditional joy possible, it is our most natural state of being.

Sometimes we may believe that other people are more powerful than we are, but this is not true. Usually, these people are just projecting a stronger or firmer idea of reality. We then start watching their movie, and may even empathically feel what they're feeling. We could describe this as losing our sense of self in empathic perception. But when we play, we honor each person and what they're experiencing, and we don't need to make it our own story. We meet them on their level as much as we can, without getting distracted from our own game.

When we begin to operate in our mastery and interact with others, it is also not uncommon to feel that we are too powerful, or that we are somehow manipulating others as if they were unconscious puppets. But this is a misinterpretation of what is happening energetically. No one is a puppet. While everyone is at different levels of consciousness within the human sphere, each of us always has some level of awareness of our own steps. There are no accidents, and the higher aspect of each of us is always in full command of our experiences. At any point, others are always capable of leaving the game we're creating.

Even if someone is choosing unconsciously—from pain or from a perspective of fear, bondage or struggle—we must still treat them as masters and honor their intelligence. To do otherwise indicates that we ourselves do not believe in our own power; we cannot say that we are masters and ultimately free if we don't acknowledge that everyone else is too. In the end, no one is ever powerless—though from some level of their consciousness they may be choosing to live as though they are. And the law of oneness shows us that no matter what an individual chooses, it is always contributing to the collective in a positive way. Though we may not be able to see it at the time, everything is always perfect.

A person with a high level of consciousness will always honor another person's choice, even if it seems to be hurting them. We cannot take away another person's ability to choose, or determine what they need to experience. In fact, attempting to take responsibility for others is often masking an unconscious desire to limit ourselves or externalize our power.

With greater self-love, we no longer worry about another person's path, because we trust in our own journey and therefore in theirs as well. We are no longer distracted by someone else's projected reality, and we place our focus back on our own conscious creation. Knowing that each person is a master will relieve us of ideas of control and remind us of our own true power to create—regardless of what another is doing.

As we expand into universal love, we begin to discover that all of our imbalances are actually a fear of love. We're afraid to open to others, to show up fully and risk being rejected by their own fear response. We become so used to fear that it becomes our default. But it is not who we are.

We have all been programmed to pull each other down to an agreed upon "maximum level of bigness." This bigness can be a maximum level of trust that we're allowed to have—with ourselves, with life, with the All That Is. But an incredible thing that happens when we really let go of the fear and embrace our bigness: people either feel more comforted by our presence, or they don't see us at all. And if they do see us and react with fear, it's simply because the fear of being too big is still within us- as all whom we encounter are our energetic mirrors.

In universal love, we no longer limit ourselves from a place of false humility or a need to be smaller than others in order to please people. We also do not feel the need to control others in order to feel safe. Instead, our safety comes from within. We deeply acknowledge everyone as masters and therefore equals, knowing that everyone can create on this level, even if they are not yet aware of it. This is freedom: freedom from the constraints of other people's needs or our own egoic selves.

The ultimate truth of higher frequencies is that no one can take our freedom from us. As creators, we all have ultimate free agency. Yet it is only from a state of expanded consciousness that we embody this freedom. We can only make choices from absolute freedom when we are conscious that we are free. When we don't know this, everything is colored with a feeling or expectation of bondage and helplessness, and we expect this disempowerment in others as well.

As we end these deep patterns of limited love and people-pleasing, we may experience loneliness or feel that we're being deserted. Loneliness is yet another sign that we are externalizing our power of creation and believe that others are the source of our happiness and freedom. Instead of interpreting this transition as loneliness, we can view it instead as a return to ourselves. What's really happening is an inner journey that can only occur when we're in our own company. We call in this alone time to remember our true essence and our magic. We begin to learn to entertain ourselves with playful activities and enjoy being in our own company. It can be an adventure!

Boundaries and Balance

As autonomous beings, we always have a choice about how we share our energy—whether we make this choice consciously or unconsciously. Sometimes, however, there are deeply imbalanced programs within us because of how we were raised or the situations we have encountered in our lives. These programs cause us to continue to create imbalanced exchanges with each other until we awaken and become more aware.

While we may be tempted to put up boundaries in an effort to change the dynamics of our exchanges, it is helpful to remember that all boundaries begin energetically and, later, as a natural result, exist in our projected world. As we shift our internal awareness and feel more self-love, our external reality also shifts to reflect this. "Protection" is really an energy. It is like having a force field around us, where the field is the powerful vibration of love and the truth of who we are. When we know that we hold and are creation energy, we will see that it is far more valuable to simply shine our light; as we do this, we propel our creation forward and in all directions, and we know that nothing that is not of this light can come in. This is the only "boundary" that is ever needed.

Barriers are a thing of the past; they do not serve us in higher-frequency consciousness. What serves us here is openness. Our new understanding of creating boundaries is to create balance where there was imbalance before, and elevate our frequency beyond the re-creation loop of old programs.

We can remember that each of us is a master, and we call each other into our lives for each exchange. As we move to create balance, we call in the people who want to learn the reciprocal aspect of that balance. And so we have a sacred exchange in which we both learn. This is always the case.

We are creating balance in so many ways right now on the planet. In this process, intimidating inner demons will come up to the surface to be loved, held and integrated into our psyche. These are apparitions; they are not actually real. Because in the fullness of integration into the All, the only thing that is "real" is love.

Romantic Love

Moving into universal love also shifts our intimate and romantic connections. It may be intimidating to love this way in our closest relationships. In our experience of human love, we have interpreted attachments as love, but attachments do not exist within these higher realms, where there is no separation and all is one.

Attachments are an aspect of the mental realm, and they have enabled us to live in and understand this world as it has been. Attachments indicate an externalization of our power. They make us think we are connected to others, but this is an illusion, a belief which cannot be carried into higher-frequency consciousness. Within the expanded consciousness and understanding of universal love, attachments wash away more and more. They don't immediately disappear, but we unravel them and see them for what they are, and we finally begin to experience what life is like without them.

Because there is no attachment in universal love, our new ways of relating may not initially feel like "romance." And since attachments are a central aspect of the mind, losing our sense of attachment can be very destabilizing. We may find it difficult to trust that we will receive everything we desire from a non-attached place.

When we create individually, we may feel highly capable and easily know our sovereignty; but when another autonomous being is involved, it can feel like the experience is out of our control. It is helpful to know that the experience is not out of our control, but the actions of the other person are. Our power, and thus our freedom and joy, are always within us. We cannot control another being, but we can command the energies of our own existence, and this creates a new reality which attracts new interactions with others.

In universal love we have a great amount of trust. We are not trusting in other people, or even ourselves; we are trusting in the law of oneness and in the All—which is infinite. This means we trust that we are also infinite, and that everyone around us is infinite. We trust in the truth of divine exchange, which means that when we put an energetic call out, it has to be met. Our safety does not come from others and attaching to them, but from trusting in ourselves and in the All, and knowing that we are continuously held and cared for. Without attachment, we come together with the motivation to play. We can learn to function without attachments by being present in our relationships as the observer.

As we anchor in this expansion, we come into a greater love for all aspects of ourselves. We transcend ideas of right and wrong, and thus the limitations of what we allow ourselves to be falls away. Because of this greater self-awareness, we are less offended when someone projects a negative vision of who we are onto us, because we understand that this means they have a negative vision of themselves—and they can only see from the perspective they've allowed themselves to expand into. The projections of others won't be an affront to us once we've expanded. When we are complete within ourselves, we do not need others to validate us, and can simultaneously have compassion for their limited projections.

Spiritual Significance of Sexual Attraction

Sexual attraction is another way in which we awaken and become more conscious through our exchanges with one another. In the experience of sexual attraction, we become aware of the powerful creation energy that we have within us, and also further understand how desire guides us to our life's purpose.

When we experience sexual attraction toward someone, we are filled with a strong desire on both biological and energetic levels. We are compelled to be around them. What sexual attraction is really doing on a spiritual level is magnetizing us to a person that carries a lesson that we want to learn.

It takes a lot of courage to face some of the lessons that, on a soul level, we deeply desire to learn. At times, if we knew beforehand the lesson we were going to learn from a person, we might run in the opposite direction to avoid learning it. The beautiful thing about sexual attraction, then, is that it engages us through our bodies instead of our minds; this helps us override our egoic worries and fears. Instead, we are motivated by our core desires, as well as by very physical reactions and chemicals flowing through us.

We always magnetize to ourselves exactly what we need. There are no mistakes. So regardless of whether someone is attracted to us, we are attracted to them, or we are mutually attracted to each other, there is a cosmic exchange that needs to occur—a soul lesson that each person involved wants to learn from one another.

When we are attracted to someone, we may have hopes about the way our connection will work out. While sexual attraction can bring us a beautiful, joyful lesson, it doesn't always turn out as we expect it to. Sometimes these soul lessons come to us in a slightly painful way—or even a very painful way. This doesn't mean that there's anything wrong; it simply means that we're playing the game of life and being human. And playing the game of life and being human inherently means that we're going to have attachments and experience emotions as a result of these attachments—emotions which are both painful and euphoric. What is most important in these experiences is to play and not deny ourselves any of the human experience.

In order for us to consciously move through any powerful attraction that arises, it's important to take a moment and just be grateful for it. Through gratitude, we become more present and therefore more able to choose. Gratitude helps us to release attachments, and become aware of the lessons that we are learning through our exchanges.

As we begin to regularly connect with others on a higher plane, we will also begin to feel a more ubiquitous physical attraction. In fact, when we begin relating to people from a higher-consciousness field, we will find ourselves attracted to many people to whom we previously were not. From this new perspective we are able to perceive a much fuller beauty in every person with whom we interact, and the fullness of that beauty ignites our bodies into attraction. This is because this higher frequency brings us into the place of universal love and helps us see one another's energetic structure, which is full of beauty and divinity. When living from an expanded perception, we are almost universally attracted to people.

This universal attraction may sound undesirable from our current perspective, but we can know that in this expanded perception, a whole new way of operating emerges as well.

When we operate from divine love we are capable of loving all others, because we have access to so much that we love within ourselves. Even if others are contracted, we can relate to them from a shared reality by recognizing those aspects in ourselves. If we are expanded, we may not choose to interact with them for an extended period of time because we want to experience our expansion. But the more expanded we are, and the more we are operating from universal love, the easier all interactions will be for us.

Sometimes our openness attracts people to us who are experiencing love from a very human place. They can't quite understand that they are falling in love with their own expanded selves by seeing it reflected in us, and they fall in love with us as a way to access this love within themselves. This can be a beautiful activation for everyone involved, and we don't need to place any judgment on it. In every circumstance, remembering and recognizing that we are all masters with different levels of consciousness will bring us into a space of universal love.

We will also meet others who are very expanded, whose power is centered within and who are conscious in their games. These are delicious interactions, wherein both beings have expanded realms within which to play and meet each other.

Relationships within universal love consciousness are so freeing. We previously operated from a paradigm in which we believed that providing for another, or even sacrificing our own truth, were tokens of our love. But that is not universal love. In universal love, we know that each person has absolute mastery over themselves and that we don't need to compromise ourselves for one another. Instead, we navigate our own experience, and feel the absolute immeasurable joy of interacting with others who are doing the same. We honor one another and do not attempt to save each other or be saved. Our safety comes from within, from knowing our own infinite nature.

We can experience greater love than we've ever known before in human form, and yes, also have it reciprocated. This may be beyond our current comprehension which is why we're being guided to release our attachments, and realize that all experiences of love are being generated from within ourselves—meaning that we are fully whole already, without another being. When we hear this, we may experience some panic, believing that if we accept our wholeness, we may never be with another. But the opposite actually occurs: we begin to attract in higher- and higher-frequency connections that even more completely fulfill our wants and desires.

Acceptance must come first, though. Without accepting ourselves as the generator of all our joys, pleasure and love, we will never be able to see this in another being, and we will never be drawn to people who are able to reciprocate it. Unless we feel it ourselves, we won't bring it in through another person. The inner calibration must happen first.

In all connections created through universal love, we pour our hearts into the interaction. We greet everyone with an open heart, we are interested in what they experience, and we love them as they are. When we interact with a person, we honor that we are being given the opportunity to witness their lifetime of unique perspectives. Can we feel what they feel and see through their eyes? What a rich experience! And what a joy it is to have a companion, or many companions in different capacities, through this process. What a joy it is to be able to play amongst others who are also enjoying their play.

As we connect with others on our journey, we may meet specific people to whom we feel a deep connection or attraction. And for one reason or another, we may find that these connections do not easily flow. There may be conflict or separation. This can make us wonder if we really do have ultimate choice in creating our world, when there is another person involved who also has choice. We may wonder, how can we close the gap between our longing and having this person in our lives?

Longing is a beautiful gift that humans have. It pulls us in the direction of our heart's desires. And it is helpful to remember that our heart's desires don't come out of nowhere—they come from our blueprint, from the very truth of who we are. When we long for a specific person, this is no different than any other desire that we may feel: the desire emerges from our blueprint, and so we can honor it as a sign, guiding us on our path. Desires—even for another person—are always, in some way, guiding us closer to our divine frequency.

The truth of quantum reality is that all choices are available to us. We can truly have anything we want, including a specific person. But we won't know what we truly want—our core-level desires—until we release our hold on what we think we want and find an inner sense of peace and joy in our fully-formed love within. In this state of self-love, our eyes are renewed, and we see new opportunities that we simply were not calibrated to see before.

And yes, it's true that our core desires will sometimes guide us to a specific person. But it takes a lot of self-awareness to know this. More often, what we really desire is the feeling we get when we are around this person. Sometimes what we desire is the experience of what that person has brought into our lives.

Therefore, when we enter into romantic partnerships, it's good to know where our desire is coming from, so that we can be in integrity with the people that we're connecting with. Do we desire them on a soul level, or do we desire them for the experience we gain, or is it all of the above? If we desire a specific person, and it comes from a place of pure desire, it is inevitable that we will be with that person, because we will never have a pure desire that can't be fulfilled.

It is normal to feel stuck when we attach our desires to a specific person. When we desire a specific person we tend to have a tight focus and project so much meaning onto them; we tend to give this person power over our happiness and joy. We make that person our god, and we use will and force to move in their direction. This dynamic sets us up for failure, because from our higher consciousness, it is not the relationship dynamic that we truly desire.

Therefore, when we feel stuck, we simply need to let go. This does not mean we are letting go of a person; instead, we are letting go of an idea that no longer serves us. This letting go is also a naturally occurring internal transformation that occurs as we ascend and continue to know that we are the source of our own happiness. We're being guided to find our own happiness and stabilize in that.

There is often a tinge of fear about releasing attachment and surrendering to our core desires, because we don't quite believe that there's more than what we already know and perceive, or that anyone can meet us where we are. We're unsure of what's on the other side of that bridge, unsure of whether something more than what we currently know exists. So often, we fear being alone, so we make sacrifices to not be alone.

We may fear that if we stop focusing on a specific person, we will drift apart from each other. We have attachments to future plans, things that we look forward to with this person. But the paradox is that everything that we desire can only occur when we release our attachments and are present in the now. When we have our eyes on higher consciousness, we naturally move in the direction that our hearts are calling us in—which may or may not be in the same direction as another person. Things get muddled when we start watching what the other does to see if it conforms to the mental paradigm that we've created about how a relationship should look.

Instead of creating relationships from a place of attachment, we can move toward our greatest joy; and if the person we desire is also moving toward their greatest joy, we can trust that we will come together if we are meant to, as designed by our divine blueprint.

When we are open to the whole Universe, we don't lose romantic love or our desire for specific people. We'll still want to be in relationships. This desire doesn't go away just because we're full of joy; rather, our fullness enhances it. And when we are full of joy and find ourselves in a relationship, we will marvel that in this whole world of billions of people, we have found each other; we will marvel that we get to play and celebrate together and be even more of what we desire together.

Universal love will feel differently than we imagine it will feel. It's true that in our happiness we will connect with many people, and many will see our light and desire to experience it; but we will meet people for whom we feel differently, and it will be clear for us. We won't be floating through a mass of people, feeling that any of them could be a romantic partner because we're so happy and enlightened. Our divine blueprint will naturally connect us with others with whom we deeply resonate. Even within universal love we can and will have partners.

It is a profound gift to find our soul-level connections, and this happens when we are vibrating within our own frequency, because we are lucid in our waking life. Whatever we choose can be ours. It's already on its way to us. The only thing for us to work on now is letting go of attachment. When we let go of attachment, we let go of a false paradigm that has been blocking us from true, divine love. We will not lose anything by becoming more of our true selves.

The connections we make with each other from the higher frequencies of universal love cause a great ripple effect of awakening. Our pure heart vibrations are shifting humanity. From our purest intentions, we all desire to have fun with each other, and we are learning how to dance together in this new, illuminated way.

The Ecstatic Body

As we expand to hold higher frequencies of light, a new awareness of our human selves begins to open. We become more alive and experience far more awareness of our bodies and all layers of our multidimensional selves. In this new awareness, we become ecstatic beings, channeling the fullness of who we are to the highest extent possible in all moments. We come to know this ecstasy of existence by honoring our body and reveling in all that we can experience and discover through this sacred vessel. The higher frequencies are the very realms of ecstasy.

To be ecstatic means to be highly present. From this presence we stream the full capacity of our light signature from the Void to animate ourselves. Ecstasy is an outpouring of love; so when we open ourselves to be an unfiltered channel of divine love, we will inherently embody and experience this state of being.

As ecstatic beings, we become the manifestation of the spontaneous and channeled frequencies of our higher self. These frequencies manifest as kriyas, or ecstatic movements in the body. They arise spontaneously and without filters, bringing our minds and bodies into a blissful state. We also see that our deep presence is our kriya; it is our creation, the God spark within us which ignites our desires and propels them to manifest in these physical realms.

As we channel this light into our human existence, our human templates act as prisms that fractalize the fullness of light frequencies into very specific codings and colors in this density realm. Each of us brings something unique through our divine energy signatures.

Ecstatic creation is like the Void laughing. It is sparkling, brilliant energy. And when our energetic channels are open and we are in pure presence within, we become the fullness of this ecstatic energy in physical form.

Our Physical Bodies

Our physical bodies are the densest expressions of ourselves. Essentially, we are light beams emanating directly from Source, and our physical bodies are the expression of that light that is furthest away from Source. We are like comets; when we see these brilliant arcs of light in the night sky, we're not actually seeing the comet but rather its tail. Likewise, when we see any creation in this physical realm, we're simply seeing the tail of the energy consciousness streaming through.

In this awakening age, we are meant to stream an even higher level of light through our bodies into these realms. But in order to have this unfiltered light streaming at such a high capacity, we need to cleanse anything that is blocking the light. This process is similar to how we experience light and shadow in these physical realms: Source sends out light to our oversoul, which acts as a prism and sends rays of light to become our human selves. If we put something in the way of that ray of light, the light becomes obstructed and casts a shadow. The only thing that keeps us from having our bodies illuminated with ecstatic energy are the filters that get in the way. The less interference there is between Source and this human expression, the more ecstatic we will become.

This is why Source light has to come through the heart and not the mind: the mind fractures and splinters our experience by trying to put it into a box. Yet this light is not something we can contain. When we allow this infinite intelligence to come through the heart and then channel it throughout the body, we become pure crystals, shining with light.

Having unfiltered, ecstatic energy running through our bodies will allow us to move through this physical reality very differently. We will even look visibly different than we did before. Our bodies and energy fields will begin to glow, and this glow will be perceptible to the human eye. This illumination happens when we activate not just the physical body but our energetic field as well.

As we become more and more illuminated, we learn to flow and move according to the currents of the frequency that we are playing within. This doesn't necessarily mean that our bodies will be animated in a specific way, or even be in motion at all; we can be sitting still and be in absolute ecstasy, for being ecstatic means being unobstructed and present in the moment. Whether we are animated or in stillness, these currents will move through us and cause a new vibration within us. We will find ourselves in blissful harmony with the specific frequencies we are channeling into our life's creation in each present moment.

Control and Dance

Our inherent nature is ecstatic. And yet, we need to learn how to allow this ecstatic energy to light up our body while also not being overwhelmed by this illumination, for the truth is, as we begin to allow this energy to flow through us, we may become so activated that it is hard to function.

It is a massively powerful experience to be in our light body. At times, ecstasy feels similar to pain because every cell is opening to allow in more light—expanding, releasing, and transmuting all that cannot vibrate with this higher quotient of light. To be filled with so much joy and playfulness is orgasmic; it can be difficult to navigate the world while holding this ecstatic energy, especially if we are emerging from deep fear programming. How can we allow our light to exist in such a strength that we are illuminated and ecstatic, and then how do we create from this place?

What often causes us to block this incredible energy from coursing through us in its fullness is the fear of our own power. We may feel uncomfortable being this bright and illuminated and worry how it will affect people around us. But anytime we hold back out of fear, we are in illusion. Operating from fear is almost like trying to see with our eyes mostly closed: we can't see fully because we're not letting everything in. Fear is just a limited perception of what is.

When we are afraid of our great power and do not trust in the All That Is, we attempt to control our experiences. Thus, our desire to hide our light is actually based on our desire for control. But as we move into the frequencies of oneness—

where we know we are all gods, masters, and sovereign light bearers—the illusion of control no longer holds up.

Control has always been an illusion. This illusion was more prevalent in previous times in human history, because there wasn't such a high level of consciousness. People would acquiesce to each other willingly, because the idea of even being an individual was perceived as going against God. Through many different incarnations, beings would agree to these "rules," believing that one was appointed by God and others were not—thus playing a game of controller and subject, master and servant. Yet even in past lifetimes in which we have seemingly had control—lifetimes of being royalty or rulers and having slaves—our interactions have always only been a dance of energies, an interplay of people giving or receiving each other's power, whether consciously or not.

The illusion of control is a mind game that is elementary in comparison to where we are now. We no longer need to operate under these outdated paradigms of control. When we see from the higher frequencies, we know that we are never truly controlling anything, but rather dancing with it all. We get to release our control in favor of this cosmic dance.

There are two ways we release our control to allow our ecstatic energy to dance through us. The first is through conscious personal work, which is our shadow work. Our shadow is what we've been using as armor against a world that seems to hurt us.

But sometimes our shadows are so heavily filtering us that we don't notice the work that needs to be done. We may have unconscious programming that has been with us for so long, it feels like an integral part of us. In these circumstances, there has to be something that acts upon us to assist us in releasing programs. Thus, the second way that we release control often occurs as a divine act, wherein our higher self steps in to assist us in surrendering. This may come in the form of a situation that makes us feel so out of control—for example a loss, a disappointment, an abrupt change—that we are pushed to surrender and release.

Releasing control usually occurs in layers. On the quantum level, as soon as we stop focusing on something, it is gone. It is instantaneous. However, in the denser physical layers of our bodies, things may take some time to clear, which can be confusing. Vestiges of old programs may still be in our field, so we may mentally refocus on them and think that we still need to clear them. But we don't need to do any more clearing. The energetic coding is already gone; it's just the mind that is holding the old programming, like an echo. The more we can recognize that the process is done, the easier the clearing through the body and psyche will be. When we cease to focus on it, we cease to recreate it.

As we learn to surrender, we begin to dance and choose consciously. And in the moment in which we grasp for control and find ourselves unable to sustain it, we can laugh at ourselves. We can laugh at the cosmic joke and at our own limiting beliefs, because we know better. We can remember that we're dancing with existence, and that everything is in command of itself.

Not having control does not confine or limit us; in fact, it frees us, because we don't need to wait for something outside of ourselves to submit to us in order to create what we desire. Instead of attempting to control, we can dance with any atom within any being. And when we know that we can dance with all of it, everything opens up for us. Even the frustrating moments become a part of the dance. Even the individuals we couldn't seem to control in lower-frequency illusions become part of the dance. Because when we learn to dance with a high level of mastery, all of the particles within everyone and everything dance with us too.

The Universe loves to dance. It is dancing all the time and is always in harmony, because it is against nothing and embraces everything. When we can get into the flow of this dance, all components of our bodies and energy begin to dance together in joyful harmony as well. This is how we can command our experience; we let go of our illusions of control and move into the truth of deep internal alignment.

When we allow this flow, every action can be ecstatic. Everything feels like it's creating itself, instead of feeling forced. There is such an ease, freedom, and joy at this level of co-creation. This universal life force energy is outside the confines of space and time, and as we begin to experience and trust it, we'll find new ways of operating within the physical realm. We'll begin to allow all of our creations to move through us in that quantum space, without our need for tight control.

Implants

Because we were born into a world with fear-based control agendas, some of us may have implants placed into our divine template. Implants are external forces that are meant to block our light and keep us filtered. But once we begin to vibrate within certain frequencies, none of these lower-frequency implements of control or fear can exist in our field.

The easiest way to clear these programs is to live in our joy. While this may seem to be an overly simplistic answer, it is the most efficient. Our practice can be to breathe into our joy and allow it to become bigger and bigger. Our work is always to focus on the light, and not to worry or be fearful about implants or agendas of control that we may not be aware of. And as we exist in ecstatic vibration, anything not of this frequency will disintegrate in our field.

This is why so many star beings of a very high frequency have come here to exist on Earth: the Earth collective needs beings whose frequency is too high to receive implants, beings incapable of having their templates taken over beyond their level of conscious choice. It needs beings with a high-level understanding of the overall game, so that even if their template were to be taken over temporarily, their soul would be too familiar with lighter frequencies to allow it to be sustained.

And even if we do succumb to some of these fear-based programs, on a higher level none of these programs are real. We are all capable of choosing to exist on this higher level. This is especially true now that the vibrations of the planet literally cannot sustain lower-frequency templates anymore, and the mental matrix is breaking. The frequencies we exist in have shifted, and the level of light now being held on the planet is unlike it has ever been before. This helps us release the long-held and unconscious programming in our templates. In order to ascend beyond the agendas of control, all we need to do is stop focusing on lower frequencies—because it is our focus on them that holds us within them.

We're doing powerful work in the world right now: we're taking a dense physical body and allowing it to become more illuminated than ever before. Our capacity to hold light is much greater than we've previously allowed ourselves to believe. But in order to hold this light, we need to clear the shadows and unmask every aspect of ourselves. We need to continue to expand in our creation and bring in more light. We are light bearers, and through this awakening, our spectrum grows until we radiate the fullness of ourselves in human form.

Becoming Crystalline

The ecstatic body is not just about being able to dance and play and be free. Our whole body and energy field are transforming to hold more light. As we shift in our consciousness, we begin to physically transform too. We are awakening to our light bodies, and thus activating into the next layer of our human structure, which is our crystalline template.

With a carbon-based body, we operate from the perception of a physical structure that's more dense. The carbon-based body and its structure are based on rigidity, cell walls and skin, barriers that seem firm to us. These components are necessary in the denser realms. But as we move into our crystalline body, we have more fluidity and -our structure is an energetic grid of light.

From these higher vibrations, we also see that the body is the totality of a collective vibrational signature—not only a physical structure, but really one big egg-shaped field of vibration. We don't see our bodies as what is contained by the barriers and the boundaries of our skin only; we see them as a full energetic system that includes our auras too. The energy emitted from us is a part of us, just on a lighter frequency.

The ecstatic realms are meant to be in continuous flow; it's when the rigidity of old programs cause us to freeze up or become paralyzed that the flow breaks and we become more dense. We can see that our programming has created an armor; when we function within these rigid programs, our energy—which normally flows ecstatically and exactly where it needs to flow—conforms to this rigidity, creating stiffness and armor in the body.

To move into and embody this layer of ourselves, we need to release our rigidity, and allow the playfulness of ecstatic energy to flow. We don't need to worry about how we can activate this amplified energy in our bodies—it is inherent to who we are. As we ascend into higher frequencies, this activation naturally occurs through the transmutation of literally every strand of our DNA, every cell of our body, every element of our physical being. Through this transmutation and shift into our light body frequency, it will be easier for us to hold higher levels of light.

We may experience some difficulty in the transmutation process, however. Part of the shift into our light bodies involves the breakdown or even complete removal of old ways of being, as a new, higher-frequency system takes over. Due to the level of change occurring, this can be overwhelming or even feel like death to the body or psyche. These shifts are happening at a quantum speed, essentially at the speed of light; meanwhile the physical body is moving through these changes slowly, within the time-based cycles of the Earth. Therefore, as these processes occur, we may experience a feeling of chaos or uncertainty in the mind and body.

Many tools are available to us to help ease our discomfort as we begin to operate in higher frequencies and make this transition. Sound, water, sunlight, dance, and breath, are all gifts we have been given to play with to help move energy through our bodies and ease this transmutation process. These tools work because they all involve an interplay between our denser human bodies and the lighter frequencies that we're becoming aware of.

Physical Body Health

As we channel more light through our systems, we may need to make physical changes. We are transitioning from a carbon-based physical system to a crystalline body structure. For this transition to be most comfortable, we need to prepare our physical bodies to hold an expanded amount of light and assist them in releasing denser carbon-based materials, which have previously constituted our dominant body structure.

While there are no rules that apply to everyone, certain practices tend to ease our transmutation process. For many of us, there is a growing tendency to eat cleaner and more plant-based foods (including a lot of greens), and less salt and processed foods. We may be drawn to foods that carry a higher vibration.

But being in an ecstatic state is about much more than just eating particular foods. In our ascension, we cross a vibrational threshold into a finer frequency. Our focus moves beyond food—because food exists in a denser frequency than where our attention is. Instead, we begin focusing on moving our energy and strengthening our toroidal field. We bring awareness to the overall flow of energy through our systems through breathwork, the opening of energy channels, and the activation of light codes. We learn that the cerebral fluid that runs through our spine is actually a form of life force energy with an electrical charge, and this electrical charge needs a certain balance. We play with energy movement and view our health from a holistic perspective that includes our vibrational well-being.

However, water continues to be important because it is helpful for both hydration and vibrational cleansing. Water is a conduit which can function on multiple frequencies. Water is a powerful tool in assisting us in the alchemical processes that are happening in our bodies. To harmonize what we put into our bodies, we can activate our food and water with the sun's light codes.

We also begin to place more awareness on our emotions and recognize what we're feeding ourselves vibrationally. We begin to see that the hormones and chemicals we activate in our bodies can either elevate us into ecstasy, or poison our health and well-being in both physical and energetic ways. As we learn to channel ecstatic energy, our bodies become much more relaxed; we hold far less tension and are able to create the chemical balance that is most harmonious for our bodies.

Movement and Flow

There is nothing that stands still in the entire existence of the All. Everything is always in motion. Taking this truth into the denser-frequency realities means that we allow energy to easily flow and shift through the body without resistance. We can't stand in its way and try to block its flow, as resistance causes a great amount of discomfort and even pain in the body. Instead of holding up barriers, we move, flow and shift the body. We dance with this ecstatic energy.

Many of our ways of being are actually subtle programs and not our bodies' natural flow. In these realms of ecstasy, however, we exist in pure presence, where our movements and actions depend on the natural cycles that we're flowing in, and not on a program.

Human bodies are meant to move in cycles across the fabric of time. Our bodies are like little animals: when we are in full presence, we inherently know our own cycles of sleep, eating, and even dance, play and free movement. And yet, we may be so deeply programmed in "appropriate" ways of being, that we block our natural physical movements, and our actions become mechanized by the mind. But through presence, we have the capacity to be in our ecstatic state continuously and consciously. We can free ourselves from these programs by allowing this energy to flow through our physical bodies through playful movement, dance and deep breathing. Our practice is to open up and give ourselves permission to fully activate the ecstatic light body through different play practices.

With deep presence, as the energy of each current moves through us, we find ourselves following these natural rhythms much more fluidly. The vibration of the energy moving through us will determine the cycle that we exist in. The unique wavelengths of energy put us into different flows, as if we're in a river with different currents.

Whenever an imbalance presents itself in our bodies, this is a sign that we're either pushing, or holding on and resisting. The nature of our discomfort will show us where we are out of balance, or out of flow with the natural cycles. This is an opportunity to surrender to the inherent rhythm that flows in and through us, and not push in one direction or another. We can release and be present.

Allowing our bodies to move with the currents flowing through us is pleasurable. When we move from our pleasure, everything we do actually feels good, and this motivates us toward the intrinsic desires of our template. Pleasure can guide us, through ease and joy, toward that which is meant for us. In these new frequencies, pleasure is our spiritual practice.

Sex

It is a truth of the quantum realms that when we place our focused attention on something, it dilates or opens, and more energy flows into it. This focus can be broad, such as divine love, or more specific, such as one point on or within the body. Our physical and auric bodies are built with many activation points which, when unlocked, open portals to powerful awakenings and higher-frequency knowledge. We can activate these portals through our focus. When these portals are open, we are able to access interdimensional information—or different wavelengths of light from a broader spectrum.

Intentional sexual practices can be very potent, because physicality is the densest and thus most focused level of reality. This powerful energy is amplified when two or more people focus together on a creation, and lovingly allow each other to help activate these points in themselves. It is especially powerful when those engaging together have learned to channel their focus through the arts of specific activation practices and physical techniques.

It is an act of divine love to learn how to harmonize frequencies while engaging sexually with another person. When beings move together in presence and pleasure, they can open so much into higher frequencies. In sacred sexual practices, there is the potential for powerful activations—such as clearing karmic lines in an instant, moving into visionary states, experiencing hyper-lucidity, and channeling ecstatic waves of energy beyond time and space.

When we are conscious, even engaging sexually with ourselves can clear our energetic field of programs, bringing us to a zero point of pure creation. And when we sexually engage with another being, we have the potential to amplify our energy and access the power of pure creation—the very power that can bring new worlds into form. In these divine connections, we are powerfully and consciously learning to harmonize, dance and co-create.

Of course, engaging in these sexual energies can be damaging as well. The act of moving with both pleasure and spontaneity inherently brings us into presence, and presence unlocks and releases programs. It can be a disharmonic exchange when we come into union with unhealed shadows and unconscious programs. Our unconsciousness allows these unlocked programs to move into the energetic template of the other person—transferring unhealed, imbalanced, and potentially toxic energy to them. If two beings are not conscious together, and an unhealed wound gets unlocked, it can be a devastating experience.

But when we bring consciousness into these sacred connections, we allow ourselves to release these unhealed shadows and programs. In the space of coming together consciously, the frequencies of divine love are opened to us, which can activate powerful healing and transmutation. Divine love frequencies are ecstatic and orgasmic—including the non-genital orgasm of our full aura being lit up. Our focus on love and our intention to bring in more light can create powerful harmonics, opening us to the higher-frequency states of pure creation. By being present in these energies with ourselves and others, we can remember the natural innocence and purity of our sexuality.

We've previously created so many barriers and structures around our love for each other that when we are this present and open in front of each other, we may feel too vulnerable and naked. Feelings of embarrassment and shame may even arise. Yet embarrassment holds us back from receiving the divine light that is our birthright, and shame is a sign that we are not accepting that we are god. Therefore, opening in this way is an important step, because holding onto these barriers will keep us in an immense amount of pain.

With presence, we can release these old programs. Freeing ourselves from these self-imposed limitations is one of the greatest gifts we can give to ourselves and one another. In our freedom, we set an example and shine our light. At our core, this is what everyone truly desires.

In these ecstatic energies, we flow with the unimaginable intelligence of the Universe, of the All That Is. We can witness the subtle interplay of the Universe responding to our every movement. We can tune into all of the tiny moments, all of the energetic exchanges, all of the barely perceptible shifts of colors. And we can watch as the colors come in like the waves of the Northern Lights, and the new painting is formed. We can flow in the present moment, observing the magic of the interplay between what has existed and what is being called in, as it creates an alchemical experience.

Return to the Garden of Eden

This Earth and all the dimensions we inhabit in this human experience are the realms of play. Play is our birthright and our purpose. It is literally what we are built for. As we become more aligned with our divine template, we naturally become filled with ecstatic frequencies, and the energy within us dances and sings. We are here on Earth to play, in all senses of the word.

At this time, our individual and collective frequencies, and the frequencies of the planet, are reaching a higher harmony that is imbued with abundance and joy. As we continue to ascend, we are returning to the frequencies of higher love, ecstatic joy, and abundance in all forms for all beings. This is our return to the Garden of Eden.

To return to the Garden of Eden means to let go of current complications and return to the simplicity of connection and oneness with the Earth. Our lives were not complicated at the origin of humanity: We knew that we were part of the Earth. Our expanded consciousness was activated, and we perceived everything like a psychedelic trip, if we were to view it from our current-day perspective. Without the paradigms and constrictions of our modern mind, we were able to witness the sacred geometric structuring of life, the light grid that our Earth exists in. We knew that we were a part of nature, that we were nature, and that all of nature spoke to us.

Our connection with the natural world has been suppressed and even demonized for so long in our human history, due to a conscious effort to exert control over humanity. The truth that nature speaks to us is threatening to forces that desire to control others—because when we are in harmony with the Earth, we are in harmony with our divine blueprint and our true power, and we know that we don't need anything external to ourselves. Our return to the Garden of Eden is our return to this harmony with every being on the planet. This is the music of existence.

Our return to the Garden coincides with a re-emergence of ancient wisdom and technologies—the knowledge of ourselves from "past" lives, and the wisdom of our ancestors, arising once again. As we awaken to higher frequencies, timelines are collapsing, and everything we have learned from all lifetimes is rapidly resurfacing and erupting into the collective consciousness.

We are bringing forth new technologies as well, for we are in a new time in the landscape of our human history. While there have been many high points throughout human history, this is a time unlike any other. We are becoming crystalline, and so we have the capacity to hold higher levels of light as well as the expanded knowledge that this light carries. New technologies include ways of healing, "whole-ing," and creating with light and sound. We come to see and know ourselves as more than human, and we align with our star ancestry. All of these higher light technologies come into our bodies and consciousness as we transmute the old structure of ourselves into new beings, channeling the full spectrum of light available in these higher-frequency realms. We become liberated within ourselves, returning to our consciousness as the cosmic fools, those who laugh with the frequencies of light as they flow through us.

Our return to the Garden of Eden is an internal, energetic shift. Since the only reality is the one emanating from within, we are in the Garden of Eden when we hold these truths within our consciousness.

Light and Sound

In our awakening to higher-frequency realms, we begin to see that all of our reality is built on light and sound vibrations. Light and sound are less dense perceptions of energy as it dances forth from Source and vibrates within the crystalline realms. We begin to see our whole reality as light and sound vibrations, witnessing the way that these two core elements interface and help transform the dense, physical part of us. In this New, light and sound become the new polarities we operate within, with light as the expansion of the yang polarity, and sound as the expansion of the yin polarity.

These frequencies are so powerful. Sound frequencies can be used to explode physical objects, and light can cut through physical matter with precision exceeding that of a scalpel. Light and sound frequencies release stagnation and transmute denser energies, enabling us to flow within higher-frequency realms. When we use these energies to heal, we can take all density within the physical body and break it up, transmuting it once again to its pure energetic form.

When we are present and flowing with the organic movement of light frequencies, we are inherently ecstatic. We desire to move with the ecstatic motion of the light pouring through us—and so we literally dance. We form mudras with our hands, create asanas with our bodies, and tone vibrations through our voices. And as we do, these movements further open the channels of our human template to hold more light.

Many of us will also begin speaking the language of light as we ascend. Though we call it a "language," it is less of a system than this word implies; it is really an energy modality, a vocal transmission of coding that unlocks different aspects of our energy body and field. This light language transmits frequencies that enhance everything we do, because it channels our personal divine frequency. We don't need a direct translation for each tone or word. Instead, just as with singing bowls or chimes, we use the sound vibration of our personal light languages to create within the energetic realms.

We can let our light codes infuse any situation or practice of which we are a part. Anytime we have a question that our mind or training can't readily answer, we can channel this light language to activate aspects of our fields that open us to higher-frequency realms. Light language channels the frequency of who we are. This is incredibly powerful, because our frequency is our purpose, and we are meant to infuse it into everything that we do.

Light language naturally moves through the brain when the mental matrix is cleared and our channels are open. We can bring ourselves to spontaneously speak light language by moving into the gamma frequency of the brain, and through other high-frequency practices.

In the ecstatic frequency realms, we easily begin to communicate telepathically as well, because our minds are clear and present. Many people think of telepathy as the need to push something out of our brain into another person's brain, but it is not this difficult. Instead, we cleanse our minds and mental fields in order to transmit signals. These energetic signals exist outside of the confines of linear time and space, so our transmissions are instantaneous. We can also telepathically communicate with people on the other side of the world, because everything is here and now.

Some people fear telepathy because they worry they'll feel exposed or too vulnerable, but the truth is we'll have a great amount of command over these transmissions. In fact, on some level we are already communicating with everything and everyone through our vibrational field. And as we learn to focus without fear or the use of forced boundaries, we'll be able to send and receive specific communication much more intentionally and effectively.

It is a powerful experience when we get to this frequency of open communication. We affect each other in ways that are beyond synchronistic, and we experience ourselves as harmonious and interwoven beyond our previous perceptions. The more we vibrate in this highly clarified frequency individually, the more we'll find harmonious connections with each other. In this higher-frequency field, we all resonate with ourselves and harmonize with each other, becoming a conscious part of the fabric of human consciousness.

Star Being Connection

When all of our channels are open to receive the full spectrum of light available to us, we activate what is known as our rainbow body. In the past, most humans were born with their chakras not fully developed, and these chakras slowly activated as they grew. However, those known as rainbow children are now arriving on the Earth with their chakras developed, creating a fully activated rainbow aura.

We may remember the prophecy of the rainbow warriors, the tales of people who are born with every light frequency activated to be able to create in these new frequencies. Now, we are all the rainbow warriors, because the full spectrum of our light bodies has been activated. But it is important to remember that we are no longer warriors, for there is no war within us and nothing to fight against. With our rainbow bodies activated we are impenetrable, because when we're complete and activated in love, nothing can harm us. There is no need for protection.

By allowing ourselves to be light bearers of a greater spectrum of the light continuum, we begin to resonate with the frequencies of our intergalactic family—the star beings who exist within higher-dimensional realms and frequencies. This rainbow body becomes the bridge of light between our human consciousness and the higher-frequency realms of our Star Family. We are being encoded with greater amounts of light to prepare us for more contact with these star beings, and to once again become conscious of the greater cosmic dance of all beings.

Many of us will begin to connect intimately with our soul Star Families, and at times we will contact ourselves on higher-frequency planes, in other star systems and in other timelines. We will begin to have visitations by our interplanetary family; and if we have already had contact with them, more will come. It will become common to bridge these connections, and to harmonize with beings who are communing with Earth to assist in our planetary ascension.

These beings are very active on the planet right now. They are assisting us in the process of activating sacred grids within the planet and unlocking our DNA to allow more light to come through. In the process, we are being showered with love. As we raise our frequency, we will find a familiarity and sense of home with these beings and energies that we know and love. Our reconnection will feel like a family reunion.

We are currently in an incredible transition, and it will continue to be more and more beautiful. Each one of us is being so activated that we may not recognize ourselves or others on the other side of these changes.

But these transitions and the resulting heightened levels of contact with our cosmic family will also be scary and uncomfortable for many people. When we open these gateways, many things that we have never seen before from our human perception will be revealed. The thought of contact with interplanetary beings may cause fear, as the energy of these beings is so different from human frequencies. There will also be many beings who look different, and this has historically caused contention on the planet. If the collective energies are not prepared throughout this greater awakening, we may see destruction to an extent that is not necessary.

The activation of our ecstatic body is necessary to open up to this contact and move beyond paradigms of fear. When we're afraid of something, we are blocked and only see part of the spectrum. By the same token, when we're not afraid of ourselves, we're not afraid of other beings. Through our activations, we will notice that, as the Bible says, "the scales have fallen from our eyes." This phrase shows the parallel between the "scales" of the reptilian lower frequency and our reptilian brain, and it refers to seeing with new eyes into multidimensional rainbow frequencies.

Being in our ecstatic body helps us open up to our full spectrum. When this light is anchored in the body we can fully feel and know our truth. As we allow more of ourselves to come in, we'll recognize our cosmic family through harmonic resonance, remembering them through the process of knowing ourselves.

We are beginning to remember that on a different layer of consciousness, we are these cosmic beings, and they are us. As we cross the Rainbow Bridge, which is the bridge of who we are, and activate the ecstatic memories in every cell in our being, we will begin to see these star beings more and more clearly. Contact will become regular and even normalized for many of us in the coming years.

We can learn to call on these beings at all times. They operate outside the realms of linear time and space, and outside the lower-dimensional operating systems that are so confining for us. Therefore, they can be present with us at any time. We simply need to gain the awareness and consciousness to not only believe this but perceive it.

Through all of these changes, our heart is still our center, the portal through which our highest self emanates. And our heart is also a stargate. We are able to open to contact with our star family by bringing our energy to a place of divine love. When we come together for this purpose, our heart frequencies are amplified and we can collectively open gateways to make contact more accessible.

We are in a process of unfolding, and each of us is becoming more finely attuned to our innate frequencies and to the truth of who we are. We will move beyond the idea that we are within one particular time and space juncture, and we will see that our consciousness can be instantly connected to all beings in all times and spaces. And as we attune in this way, more and more contact with our star family will occur.

Laughter and the Cosmic Fool

When we exist in a sixth dimensional consciousness, we are in the realms of pure play. We are far beyond the confines of dualism and deeply recognize that life is a game, a joyful expression of creation within multiple layers of consciousness. This is the realm of the cosmic fool, wherein we know that we are both the All and the Nothing, and we can experience the interplay of these cosmic forces at once.

We can recognize people who understand the play of creation by their laughter. They are laughing through life because they get the cosmic joke and can hear the music and the song of divine creation.

Laughter is a way to awaken our happiness and play, and is one of the key elements of the ecstatic body. It is a gift we were given that is unique to the human experience. Laughter registers at a high vibratory rate that we can feel, and it transmutes denser energies in the body. The spontaneous eruption of laughter sends a vibration throughout our body that breaks up stuck areas and allows light to flow more easily through our field. This is like plucking a guitar string; it is a vibrational tickle whose reverberation connects us with a deeper inner wisdom.

Through inner stillness we can access a deeply organic, ecstatic laughter. It is important to know that stillness is an internal frequency, not necessarily a lack of physical motion. Stillness is presence. This stillness is not only found in meditation, but also through profound presence with existence. Deep stillness engenders a tickling—the kriya of cosmic energy through the body—and this tickling is what activates us into spontaneous, organic laughter.

When we connect to this higher-frequency current of the All That Is, we begin to see that we're all cosmic fools, playing our part in this divine orchestration of light, creating silly things for ourselves to loop and then discover.

In this life, we have been taking ourselves so seriously. And it is indeed important to honor our divine callings, to honor our great power as gods on Earth—but not to the point of seriousness. We are stellar creations, endlessly spiraling into eternity! This is a cause for wonder as well as laughter, for what other response could we possibly have to the fact that we're embodying such an expression? Anytime we wonder, "Where's the laughter? Where's the play?" we can laugh at ourselves for forgetting that it's right here, right now, and that not only are we playing a joke on ourselves, we also are the joke. And what a funny game we are playing, forgetting that we are the All.

We are fools for playing the game, first unconsciously, and now coming into consciousness. We are fools in blocking the light that we seek. Abundance and all that we could ever desire are here for us now, if we can learn not to fight the New that's coming in. Isn't it funny that we often fight things that are actually for our benefit, because we perceive them as new, and therefore a threat to our safety?

We're trying to be fed by a full spectrum of light now. As much as possible, we can relax the resistance and let our hearts sing to us; our hearts will communicate how to navigate these new realms.

We are moving into higher and higher frequencies of light now. We are becoming the beings that we always knew we could be--who we are written within. Higher-than-ever levels of light are available to us now, and it is up to each of us to choose these levels of light, which means to believe in our worthiness.

It is important to allow ourselves time to release the structures internally that have been built to block us from the All That Is. We can find comfort in remembering how loved we are by all of the beings on these higher frequencies, where there are no conditions on love; there is no need to be conditional, because they have no need to keep themselves safe. That is why so often love becomes conditional in our human sphere—because of the idea of the need for safety. But we can move beyond that now. We can allow ourselves to be loved in our fullest capacity, and to emanate this love into the world and into all of our creations. And everything is our creation. We are powerful creators—and we would do well to remind ourselves of this often.

The Garden of Eden is open to us now. The Garden is in the heart. It is the heart. Because in the heart, there is no opposition, and all things can exist. Therefore, the heart space streams the codes of pure abundance. The light of pure creation is flowing and emanating more strongly than ever before. The fullness of this light assists us in connecting with our star family—beings who exist in many different dimensional realities and who are ready to begin collaborating with us now.

There are so many changes occurring. If we can see this life as a game and play with it as such, we will find ourselves dancing in the harmony of all of creation. Let us find presence and learn to navigate from this place, so that we can play in these frequencies.

May the light of our beingness dance within all of us. May we all know ourselves as ecstatic beings on the playground of Earth.

Acknowledgements

I'd first like to express my profound gratitude for my editor, Molly Clinehens, for your dedication and tenacious desire for clarity, and for honoring the spirit of the transmissions on each page of this book (and for even editing this section!) And for your friendship.

To my family, you are each soul mates, and I am so grateful to play the roles we get to play with each other together in this life. I would especially like to express love and gratitude to my mom, who taught me how to love without conditions, and how to play with life in the most joyful ways!

Helia Aurora, you are so incredibly magical. I'm grateful for the play we've had together in many lifetimes and forms. (Screams in Mayan!)

Asia Wolf, thank you for being the match to my divine template, and for all I've learned and continue to learn through our connection.

Wind and Ocoa, you are my family forever and I love you both.

Tabi Howard, thank you for playing with me, and teaching me new ways to play in this beautiful world.

Dianne Prado, thank you for bringing me love and acceptance during many discouraging moments in this process, and informing me that my real work in creating this book is to discover what play is not. That was profoundly clarifying for me.

Amber Dowell, thank you for opening the space for me to connect with this earth and her many medicines.

Charlotte Dietz, thank you for your multidimensional wisdom, and for all the playful channelings we shared as this book was being created.

Eileen Fox-Quamme, thank you for showing up in perfect timing and for asking the perfect questions. I am grateful for your brave and playful spirit!

To Dayna De Leon Perez, for channeling for me, "I keep hearing it's already done!" And now I understand that message. It is all already done.

To the ladies, Bonnie Schwartz, Gigi Mills, Lili Pierrepont, Penina Meisels: thank you for sitting with me during so many channelings that ended up in this book; and to Michael Bergt for your friendship and for introducing me to this circle.

Mark, you are a great friend to have, and wonderful to channel for. Thank you for the many inspirations which appear in this book.

And I would like to express so much gratitude for the book launch presenters: Monique Gomez, Amy Anthony, Julia Leible, Barbara Caraballo, and Robin Bailly. The wisdom that each of you bring is so powerful, and I am honored to have you in my world.

A special thank you to Luiza Deftu for your support and assistance in my work. You are a gift and a wonderful friend.

To all of the members of the True Creator Community, past, present, and future. I love being a part of your lives, and having you as a part of mine.

And to the clients for whom I have channeled, whose questions created the channeled stream of consciousness that led to many passages in this book, thank you!

My gratitude to the sacred plants, the consciousness of ayahuasca, tobacco, rose, and cacao.

Infinite gratitude to my Star family, the Andromedan council, the guidance of the Annunaki, Council of Nine, and countless other beings who don't have a need to be named because they don't have an ego :D But whom I honor just the same.

To my human ancestors, for your personal joys, pains, and evolution. Thank you for being writers of the code.

To each of you, thank you for playing such a divine game with me.

About the Author

Allison Holley is an Andromedan starseed, channel, and author of the books <u>The Era of the True Creator</u> (2018) and <u>Ecstatic Playground</u> (2023). After experiencing a profound awakening in 2012, Allison began spontaneously channeling and receiving visions of the world to come. She left her former life to integrate these higher frequency downloads, and eventually began teaching and channeling for others. Allison now offers channeled transmissions, activations, and guidance worldwide, to assist in our current global awakening.

To learn more, please visit: www.allisonholley.com.

Also, if you enjoyed this book, please leave a review!